Praise for MADE

"My friend David Kim has given the church a unique and special contribution. His insights on community and the great ache of loneliness in our time are some of the best I've found. This is a book I will be passing out to all my friends. I hope you enjoy it as much as I did."

—JOHN MARK COMER, FOUNDER OF PRACTICING THE WAY
AND *NEW YORK TIMES* BESTSELLING AUTHOR OF *THE RUTHLESS
ELIMINATION OF HURRY*, *LIVE NO LIES*, AND MORE

"Infused with practical wisdom and personal narratives, *Made to Belong* invites us to be honest about our loneliness and prepares us to build meaningful connections. What a timely book that encourages us to prioritize each other!"

—JOHN HUH, VICE PRESIDENT OF STUDENT LIFE AND DEAN
OF CHAPEL, PRINCETON THEOLOGICAL SEMINARY

"We have an epidemic of loneliness. Many of us want to connect but don't know how. That's why I'm so grateful for David Kim, who offers biblical wisdom and best practices to build deep and meaningful relationships. One of the things I loved about *Made to Belong* is its emphasis on how these practices shape the people we become, as David vulnerably shares insights he's learned the hard way through his own most intimate relationships and years of shepherding spiritual formation in church community."

—JOSHUA RYAN BUTLER, LEAD PASTOR OF REDEMPTION TEMPE;
AUTHOR OF *BEAUTIFUL UNION* AND *THE SKELETONS IN GOD'S CLOSET*

"Written thoughtfully from his personal journey to belonging, David gives us a road map to navigate our own desire for meaningful community and to the ways we help and hinder our progress. His writing is warm, approachable, nuanced, and challenging. It will be a meaningful resource for my own growth and for groups that I lead."

—TERI O'NEEL, SPIRITUAL DIRECTOR AND
EXECUTIVE DIRECTOR OF WELLSPRING

"We're in an isolation and loneliness crisis. Technology's promise of a global utopian village has proven a farce and we find ourselves moving further apart, losing our ability and aptitude for meaningful connection. David Kim's book is both a pastoral and prophetic call back home to belonging. I've seen David's life, up close and personal. This book is not just a set of ideas; it's a story lived and continuing to be lived by a deeply devoted follower of Jesus who's felt the pain of loneliness and has taken the long journey toward meaningful community. I can't recommend this book enough."

—JAY Y. KIM, LEAD PASTOR OF WESTGATE CHURCH;
AUTHOR OF *ANALOG CHURCH* AND *ANALOG CHRISTIAN*

"I resonated deeply with this book because we are all born with the innate truth that it is not good to be alone. It's only been exacerbated by the Fall, the centuries of human history, and the recent global pandemic. I love how this book brings together David's personal journey, the community life at WestGate Church, current research, and biblical insights. Thank you for showing us the practical steps out of loneliness and into belonging."

—DJ CHUANG, AUTHOR OF *MULTIASIAN.CHURCH: A FUTURE
FOR ASIAN AMERICANS IN A MULTIETHNIC WORLD* AND
COFOUNDER OF CHRISTIAN ASIAN MENTAL HEALTH

"David's new book on belonging answers this generation's longing for connection. *Made to Belong* approaches the topic of community from a holistic view integrating Scripture, psychology, and mental health. It's the best book out there on this topic."

—WILL CHUNG, LEAD PASTOR OF BELOVED CHURCH

"David invites you to not only reflect on your personal experience of belonging but also proclaims that a healthy sense of belonging starts with understanding Jesus' teachings. David's honest and humble self-reflections throughout the book are culturally sound and deeply relatable. The five practices he shares from his deep study of belonging are timely and life-giving to anyone who is searching for true belonging."

—ANGIE KIM, ASSISTANT PROFESSOR OF COUNSELING,
GORDON-CONWELL THEOLOGICAL SEMINARY

"Such a timely book for the disconnected, lonely world we live in currently. This book is biblically sound, well researched, and packed with rich insights that will prove to be a game-changer for cultivating authentic, meaningful relationships."

—JEFF HYUN, PASTOR AND FOUNDER OF BARNABAS & CO.

"The COVID-19 pandemic has amplified what was already lurking in our midst. The facade of pseudo-connectedness could no longer veil the isolation and loneliness, manifesting in anxiety and depression, perhaps the greatest diseases of our modern-day times. In *Made to Belong*, David Kim offers an untainted and profound antidote to the ceaseless pursuit of the next big hype in our futile attempts to fill the void. He invites us to see what can unfold when we prioritize showing up as our full, unadulterated selves to disclose with vulnerability, listen with intentionality, and sit in the pain together with authenticity."

—JOSEPHINE M. KIM, FACULTY AT HARVARD UNIVERSITY,
LICENSED MENTAL HEALTH COUNSELOR, AUTHOR, SPEAKER,
AND FOUNDER OF MUSTARD SEED GENERATION

MADE TO BELONG

FIVE PRACTICES FOR CULTIVATING COMMUNITY IN A DISCONNECTED WORLD

DAVID KIM

NELSON
BOOKS

An Imprint of Thomas Nelson

Published in Nashville, Tennessee, by Nelson Books, an imprint of Thomas Nelson. Nelson Books and Thomas Nelson are registered trademarks of HarperCollins Christian Publishing, Inc.

Thomas Nelson titles may be purchased in bulk for educational, business, fundraising, or sales promotional use. For information, please e-mail SpecialMarkets@ThomasNelson.com.

Unless otherwise noted, Scripture quotations are taken from the ESV° Bible (The Holy Bible, English Standard Version°). Copyright © 2001 by Crossway, a publishing ministry of Good News Publishers. Used by permission. All rights reserved.

Scripture quotations marked NIV are taken from The Holy Bible, New International Version°, NIV°. Copyright © 1973, 1978, 1984, 2011 by Biblica, Inc.° Used by permission of Zondervan. All rights reserved worldwide. www.Zondervan.com. The "NIV" and "New International Version" are trademarks registered in the United States Patent and Trademark Office by Biblica, Inc.°

Scripture quotations marked NKJV are taken from the New King James Version°. Copyright © 1982 by Thomas Nelson. Used by permission. All rights reserved.

Scripture quotations marked TLB are taken from The Living Bible. Copyright © 1971. Used by permission of Tyndale House Publishers, Inc., Carol Stream, Illinois 60188. All rights reserved.

Any internet addresses, phone numbers, or company or product information printed in this book are offered as a resource and are not intended in any way to be or to imply an endorsement by Thomas Nelson, nor does Thomas Nelson vouch for the existence, content, or services of these sites, phone numbers, companies, or products beyond the life of this book.

ISBN 978-1-4002-3508-7 (audiobook)
ISBN 978-1-4002-3507-0 (eBook)
ISBN 978-1-4002-3496-7 (TP)

Library of Congress Control Number: 2022948493

Printed in the United States of America

23 24 25 26 27   LSC   10 9 8 7 6 5 4 3 2 1

*To my wife Nina—Thank you for loving me so well
and creating a safe place where I can belong.*

*And to my men's group (TNI), where I am learning
what it means to fully experience this book.*

Contents

Introduction: We Are Losing Our Ability to Belong xi

PART ONE: WHY BELONGING IS SO HARD

1. The False Connection Cycle 1
2. Barriers to Belonging 19

PART TWO: HOW BELONGING IS POSSIBLE

3. Practice #1: Priority
   Let's Talk About Our Commitment Issues 41

4. Practice #2: Chemistry
   The Difference Between Clique and Click 61

5. Practice #3: Vulnerability
   Lowering the Wall of Shame for Connection 79

6. Practice #4: Empathy
   Supporting Others Well in a Self-Absorbed World 107

7. Practice #5: Accountability
   The Necessary Road to Christlikeness 135

CONTENTS

**PART THREE: HOW BELONGING DEEPENS OUR DISCIPLESHIP
TO JESUS**

   8. Being Fully Known and Truly Loved 159

   9. The Gift of Isolation 165

  10. Cultivate Belonging in Christian Community 183

Conclusion: Discerning to Stay or Move On 199

Acknowledgments 205

Notes 209

About the Author 216

Introduction

WE ARE LOSING OUR ABILITY TO BELONG

I t was one of the most painfully honest letters I had ever received, and it came from my best friend.

Dear David,

Hey man, I can't believe you are going off to college! We've known each other ever since you moved here from Korea and we had some good times. But if I'm honest, you only care about yourself, and I don't think you know me well. It's mainly been one way. I feel like I'm doing most of the work in this friendship, and I don't think you care about me that much. I want to say that you aren't a great friend, and I certainly don't want to be best friends with you as you go off to college. Something really needs to change in you.

Paul was the first friend I made when I moved to the United States. His family lived right upstairs from us in a split-level house on Long Island. He was a year younger than me, but with our love for basketball, video games, and collecting sports and Pokémon cards, we instantly became best friends. I had much to learn about American culture, language, music, what to wear— Paul taught me everything. Since we attended the same school and church and lived in the same duplex, Paul was my guide in this new land.

I'd loved my time in Korea. I didn't want to leave my school, church, and friends, but my parents often spoke about this fantastic land filled with better opportunities, better education, and a better life. I believed that our lives would improve in America. We would have a bigger house, live on less-crowded streets, learn English, and I could get into a college respected by the world. So late one winter, in pursuit of the American dream, our family packed everything we owned in huge, wheeled, expandable duffel bags the size of washing machines.

When I arrived in the United States, however, this dream took a different turn. My ten-year-old self could not have been more unprepared for this version of the so-called American dream. I quickly experienced what it meant to be a stranger. I didn't speak the language. I didn't understand the culture. I could not relate to anyone. I was completely alone. I was in America, but I faced constant reminders that I wasn't *really* American. This disorienting lack of connection put me on a desperate search for belonging. Like most kids, I needed a place where I could feel loved, where it was safe to be *me*.

While I was acclimating to the new world of America, America and the world were being changed by the internet—and I became enamored with all that it offered. It was a world I could figure out and navigate on my own. It was a place where no one could see that

I was different. I escaped into online multiplayer games, spending hours playing *Counter-Strike* and *StarCraft*. I grew to love the online world more than the actual world. Sometimes when Paul would run downstairs to watch a movie, play cards, or shoot hoops with me, I would turn off the lights in my house to make him think I wasn't home. It was easier for me to make a digital connection than to face rejection in the real world.

The truth is, Paul and I were in the same spaces a lot of the time—school and church and our neighborhood—but I didn't know how to be a true friend. Even if I sometimes had twinges of guilt about how I treated Paul, I didn't know how to deal with all the complex feelings of being a stranger in a strange land.

Then, the summer after my senior year, as I was getting ready to move to Boston for college, Paul handed me that letter.

When I read it, I knew he was right. It was painful to admit, but I hadn't been a good friend. Paul had offered *belonging* through the gift of friendship in America, but I didn't know how to receive and experience it. I was frustrated by that and, despite Paul's best efforts, I was still very lonely. I felt unseen, unknown, and unloved. I felt disconnected from people around me, misunderstood, and left out. Looking back, I realize I was searching for answers to questions like these:

- Who will accept me for who I am?
- How do I create meaningful friendships?
- What does it mean to be loved, and how do I create a loving relationship?

I've spent much of my adult life trying to understand loneliness and what to do about it, and this book holds the fruit of my efforts.

I've discovered that belonging—one of our fundamental human needs—is the best way to overcome loneliness.

Psychology Today defines loneliness as a "state of distress or discomfort" caused by a "gap between our desire for social connection and our actual experience of it."[1] It often has less to do with others' physical absence and is more about *emotional* or *psychological* distance, which is why an extrovert can know and interact with many people and still feel lonely. Or why I could have a best friend like Paul and still be fundamentally disconnected and lonely.

Loneliness affects all groups, regardless of gender, race, or age: introverts, extroverts, influencers, counselors, pastors, single people, married couples. We all want to

be seen,
be known, and
be included.

We all need *belonging*—because we were made to belong.

WE ARE *ALL* LONELY BUT DON'T WANT TO BE

"Hey! Ching-Chong!"

I definitely heard that name more than once, and a million others like it. One time I was walking down the stairs in middle school and someone yelled "Spoon Dropper!"—which was weird because I had not dropped any spoons. I found out later he called me that because when a metal spoon is thrown down the stairs, it makes the *ching ching ching ching* sound. Junior high can be painful for everyone, but it was brutal for me. Even when the other kids weren't calling me names, they made slanted eyes or Kung Fu motions in my direction as they laughed.

As a newcomer to America, I never wanted to stand out. I simply wanted to fit in. I hated it when people noticed my accent and tried to correct me. I can still hear the giggles in the classroom when my Korean name 장현 "Jang Hyun" was pronounced during attendance. For the first time, I began to be ashamed of my own name. And these comments repeatedly reinforced my new reality: I was an outsider and I didn't belong.

I especially dreaded lunch period. There were so many anxious thoughts running through my mind: *Who do I sit with? Will anyone invite me to their table? Can I stand another torturous lunch time sitting alone?* The pain of loneliness was too much for this ten-year-old to bear. I sometimes ate my lunch inside dirty elementary school bathroom stalls. I had to weigh what was more bearable— loneliness or a smelly bathroom? Smelly bathroom won almost every time.

Even if you are not an immigrant, you likely know what it feels like to be disconnected, unseen, and unknown. Maybe you moved to a new city, started a different job, or joined a new church community. Maybe close family and friends have moved away or loved ones have passed away. Your disability, level of education, race, ethnicity, economic and marital status, gender, political views, and faith have made you invisible or even discriminated against. Perhaps you have realized that you haven't invested in many deep friendships throughout your life.

As I write this, in the midst of the COVID-19 pandemic, most of us have experienced for the first time shelter-in-place (SIP). We isolated ourselves from others in order to slow down the spread of the virus. We only left the house for essential things like groceries or visiting a doctor for an emergency.

Many people struggled with that isolation. Even introverts like my wife couldn't handle it after a week (though it may very well be that she was tired of being with *me* the whole time). We began to realize, if we hadn't already, how essential our *belonging to others* is for our human survival and well-being. It reminded us that God did not design humans to be alone (Genesis 2:18).

This pandemic unleashed a flood of loneliness, revealing that we were already lonely but didn't fully realize it until the pandemic. Many of us are just waking up to it.

In 2018, Cigna's research showed nearly half of Americans reported sometimes or always feeling alone (46 percent) or left out (47 percent). One in four Americans (27 percent) rarely or never feel as though there are people who really understand them. Two in five Americans sometimes or always feel that their relationships are not meaningful (43 percent), and that they are isolated from others (43 percent).[2] That is data before COVID-19. Sadly, 2020 data shows an overall increase in loneliness to 61 percent.[3] I can't even imagine what these numbers would be now.

We've had the opportunity to honestly examine who our community is, asking:

- Who are my people?
- Where do I experience meaningful belonging?
- Why is it so difficult to find belonging?
- How many people know me well?
- Why do I have relationships yet still feel alone?
- How do I cultivate soul-connecting spiritual friendships?

If we are honest, we are losing our ability to build meaningful connections and friendships. As we continue to live in this world with frequent surface-level interactions, we find ourselves settling for distracting substitutes when really we long for more belonging. We just have no idea how to get there. We are slowly, if not already, becoming people living in greater anxiety, fear, and pride.

In other words, our problem is inevitable.

We live in a culture of disconnection, which leads to loneliness and isolation. It's easy to neglect God's gift of friendships and community. Therefore, we are losing our ability to belong and becoming more self-absorbed and anxious individuals.

This should not come as a surprise. When we are left to ourselves, we naturally drift away from God and others. In the Bible, the apostle Paul told us that in the last days "people will be lovers of self, lovers of money, proud, arrogant, abusive, disobedient to their parents, ungrateful, unholy, heartless, unappeasable, slanderous, without self-control, brutal, not loving good, treacherous, reckless, swollen with conceit, lovers of pleasure rather than lovers of God" (2 Timothy 3:2–4). *Ouch*. The warning has been there all along.

WHY I WROTE THIS BOOK

Global disruptions and massive changes throughout the pandemic and the digital age are ushering in unique challenges to our relationships and faith. So many of us are feeling weak, confused, and stalled in our faith journey. Some of us have tried (and are still trying!) to fight against disconnection and isolation, but even in our best approach to belonging, we often find ourselves frustrated and somehow still lonely.

In my twenty-plus years of pastoral ministry in various contexts, I've heard about and regularly encountered people struggling with belonging, including myself. It goes something like this:

IN YOUR FAMILY: You share a last name on paper. You legally belong but still feel out of place and uncared for.

IN YOUR MARRIAGE: You care for your spouse but you still feel lonely and long for a deeper connection.

IN YOUR WORKPLACE: You are part of the team but you still feel unseen.

IN YOUR FRIEND GROUPS: You are laughing and having a good time but are wishing for more meaningful conversations.

IN YOUR COMMUNITY: You appreciate where you live but find yourself left out or even feeling shamed for being "different."

IN YOUR CHRISTIAN COMMUNITY: You participate and yet still can't find community.

So . . . *what are we missing?*

When I first came to America, I was an outsider. I needed to figure out how belonging worked for my own well-being. And I realized that I wasn't the only one with this problem. So many others experienced it too.

The Bible shows the significance of belonging from the earliest parts of our human story—how God designed us to be relational beings, made to belong to God and others. We are created *in* community—"let us make man in our image" (Genesis 1:26)—and *for* community—"it is not good that the man should be alone" (Genesis 2:18). Yet sin brought separation in all forms of relationships. We became self-centered and divisive—in biblical terms, belonging to ourselves, the Evil One, and the world, living in opposition to God's ways. While the Bible declares, "The earth is the LORD's, and everything in it, the world, and all who live in it" (Psalm 24:1 NIV), we may prefer to belong to someone else (self, the Evil One, the world). By God's grace, our story does not end there. Through the finished work of Jesus on the cross, reconciliation of all broken relationships—with both God and others—was made possible. And the Bible provides incredible wisdom and hope as we navigate belonging in a fragmented and disconnected world.

When I finally accepted that I was living a disconnected and lonely life, I looked back and realized that I'd moved more than twenty-two times. I had to constantly navigate new friends, cultures, communities, neighbors, and churches. Though I maintained surface-level connections over the years, I'd never experienced deeper layers of belonging. I hid behind busyness, a language barrier, and the pastorate. I also carried some real fears about getting close to others.

And if I'm honest, I also resisted both the gift and hard work of belonging. I am grateful for my wife, Nina, as well as professors, pastors, coaches, friends, my spiritual director, and my therapist, who have come alongside me and modeled safe spaces and key elements for belonging that I am now able to articulate in this book.

They enabled me to start openly sharing my journey of loneliness as a Korean American Christian male in America,[4] which led to writing my children's book dealing with change.[5] It is a book I wish I had growing up as I was processing and navigating through loneliness and striving for belonging in the midst of life's changes. It's been a joy to hear how parents are using the book to have conversations with their kids about how they're really doing, and to read it together with my two daughters as well.

As God showed me more about belonging, He did so in such unexpected places and events, including a unique group of busy Silicon Valley Christian men, who have been meeting consistently every Tuesday night for the past twenty years. In the midst of that intentional community, I began asking, What makes belonging possible in this group? How does it work?

All of this culminated in applying my love of research, theological training,[6] and pastoral ministry experience to survey more than thirteen hundred people as part of my role as the discipleship and formation pastor at WestGate Church in Silicon Valley. We wanted to create spaces of real belonging, community, and transformation, so we asked: Are Christians experiencing deep belonging on a consistent basis? Why or why not? Is the small group model providing meaningful belonging? What do we see in the Bible about it? And what about in psychology and neuroscience? Are there any consistent elements it requires? And how does our journey of belonging deepen our discipleship to Jesus? Genuinely, it's been an education and an honor to hold hundreds of people's stories.

To my surprise, five common practices came up over and over—five clear steps to help navigate the complexities of human relationships. The practices are rhythms for centering and grounding us and keeping us from drifting away from what matters most. We will explore how these practices help us stand in resistance to bad theology and half-truths in our cultural moment that are detrimental to our journey of belonging.

It is challenging to show up and honestly deal with our inner fears and failures, including those we've adopted from society. But belonging is so important to our overall well-being and spiritual growth that leaving it to chance and luck alone in order to find meaningful belonging where we are fully seen, known, and loved now seems to me both careless and ineffective. Belonging runs counter to self-sufficiency, isolation, loneliness, and a breakdown of mental and emotional health. Ultimately, it offers a safe place for real transformation.

We won't change unless we feel *safe*. And real belonging offers that safety. We know this well from belonging to Jesus. We are safe and secure in His unchanging love, and from that anchored place we can face what today and tomorrow will bring. Healthy belonging leads to becoming the person God intended us to be.

Despite that letter from Paul, he and I kept in touch when we went off to college, and even when we moved across the country. But we have never talked about his letter. We were best men at each other's weddings and saw each other become fathers, working and serving our families. As I finished writing this chapter, I decided to give him a call. I told him I'm writing a book about belonging, and that there was a small part about him. I read some of it, including the letter that he wrote, and to my surprise, he didn't recall writing it at all, which I suppose is a good thing. We both chuckled our way through it. And I thanked him for being there for me and offering belonging when I needed it most. I said it meant much more than he could ever realize. Even when I couldn't be the friend he deserved, Paul stuck by me and continued to offer belonging, and I'm so grateful.

Belonging matters.

In fact, it may matter more than anything.

Part One

WHY BELONGING
IS SO HARD

W
e crave life-giving relationships and community yet realize
it is difficult to find and cultivate them. So instead of
choosing genuine connections, we settle for less. And in the process,
we are losing our ability to belong even more.

But we don't have to.

Let's begin by learning the common pitfalls of belonging that
hinder us and by gaining greater self-clarity for our journey to cultivating community.

Chapter 1

The False
Connection Cycle

R efresh.
Again.
And again.
Seven—I mean seventy-seven—more times.

I'm checking how many "likes" I have on a beautiful post I wrote about my Christian faith. I want to know who is reading and affirming my incredible wisdom. As the count gets higher and higher, I am getting nervous. *What if I only get a hundred "likes"? What will others think of me then? Did my pastor like my post? If not, why? Maybe he is busy and has not been on the platform yet. Let me check his page to see if there have been any recent movements. Or maybe he disagrees with my thoughts.*

If you've experienced this situation before, you understand how distressing it can be. One day I was watching *The Social Dilemma* and heard the inventor of the "like" button on Facebook (now Meta), Justin Rosenstein, sharing that he created it as a tool to create *positivity* among its users.

Positivity!

It makes a lot of sense. It's a "thumbs up" button. How could it be harmful?

But little did he know it would have the opposite effect for millions of users. Rather than feeling positivity, many of us have experienced anxiety and insecurity while staring at our latest post, longing for more people to "like" or affirm who we are.

This platform and others promise real connection, community, and belonging. But do they actually provide that? If we are not careful, the very tools that are supposed to help us *like* each other can have the opposite effect. The constant clicking of "refresh" can be exhausting. We need to slow down a bit and evaluate honestly. We need to see if these tools are actually working.

WE SETTLE FOR LESS

Throughout my life, instead of facing the fear and pain all that isolation and loneliness caused within me, I pursued connections that promised belonging. Little did I know that I was settling for many false connections to cope with my need to belong. Real belonging takes a lot of work. It is often easier to choose false connections because they do not require commitment, sacrifice, or vulnerability. They are cheap substitutes that do not satisfy our deeper longings. In turn, they cause more anxiety and loneliness.

I didn't know at the time, but I was trapped in what I now call the *False Connection Cycle*.

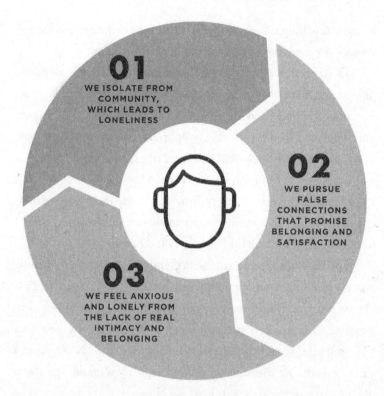

THE FALSE CONNECTION CYCLE

Here is how the False Connection Cycle works:

First, *we isolate ourselves from community, which leads to loneliness.* A variety of factors prompt us to self-isolate. Maybe we had a negative experience with someone—gossip, abuse, betrayal, neglect, insecurity, lack of safety and care (just to name a few). Or perhaps we are in a busy season where we are juggling work and family responsibilities. Maybe we are exhausted and burned out from the never-ending demands on our time and energy by life and difficult relationships. Some struggle with fear of rejection and are worried that taking a risk on a person or community will lead to more crushing disappointment. Or maybe—though it's hard to admit—we love to be independent and self-sufficient.

The second step in the False Connection Cycle is that *we pursue false connections that promise belonging and satisfaction*. Growing up, I would often feel tired after physically and emotionally engaging with Paul, so I would turn off my lights, hoping he wouldn't come down to play. I also felt very insecure. My food smelled different, so I ate alone. My English was terrible, so I spoke less and less and stayed away from others. Everything that made me unique, different, and special became my source of shame and isolation. And I hated relying on others for help. I was too proud.

The most visible and consistent reminder that I didn't belong was my clothing. In some ways, every kid feels the pressure to wear the cool clothes that everyone else is wearing. As an immigrant, however, I felt that pressure even more. In the nineties in New York City, my peers wore expensive North Face coats and JNCO jeans. I didn't even know where to get those things. How could I go about asking my parents for a $200 jacket? Nowadays, the way to fit in is to look and be *different*, but it's still the same human longing for belonging. The fashion industry is selling us belonging and we fall for it every time.[1]

Think about a time in your life when you felt pressure to fit in or belong. Did you change yourself—not staying true to who God created you to be—all in the name of fitting in? We show a falsified version of ourselves because we are afraid that who we are isn't enough. Or we only reveal a toned-down version of ourselves because we're afraid that who we are is too much.

In our desire to survive, many of us learned to "code switch," which involves adjusting our style of speech, appearance, behavior, and expression in a way that will optimize the comfort of others in exchange for fair treatment, greater opportunities, and belonging.[2] This happens when an underrepresented individual faces a dominant group, for example: a woman in a room with all male leaders to "gain respect" by taking on more work than she has to or a black man changing his verbiage and tone to sound more "white" in interviewing for a job. This can be taxing on our mental health, being hypervigilant in constantly "reading the room" to be "appropriate" and even compromising our own values not to rock the boat, which can be more damaging to our souls.

Certainly there are good reasons to be adaptable and flexible in our relationships with other people. Learning to contextualize in communicating to others is relational wisdom. Even the apostle Paul talked about becoming all things to all people, to win people over to the truth of the gospel so that they may belong to God's family and be seen for their true selves (1 Corinthians 9:19–23). But the pressure to fit into society is different. Striving to become all things to all people in an effort to win acceptance into a group with unrealistic or unfair standards of who we should be is exhausting.

There are so many opportunities for *false connections*, which are superficial relationships that don't actually require vulnerability or sacrifice and therefore cannot satisfy our deep longing to belong. For example, on average, we spend 3 hours and 15 minutes on our phones, and 2 hours and 24 minutes on social media every day.[3] Pornography is a replacement for real love and connection. In one year, the most popular pornography site logged more than 5.8 *billion* hours of views.[4] Facebook tells me I have nearly two thousand "friends," but I think I can count only twenty with whom I share meaningful conversations and significant engagements. Granted, I am thankful for all the ways in which social media makes our world a better, more connected place. For instance, one of my closest friends found his biological mother through Facebook and reunited with her last year! But more often than not, social media only offers the *promise* of connection. It cannot actually deliver relationships with real weight or offer satisfaction for the soul's deeper longings.

This has real consequences, especially in how we think about relationship building. We can instantaneously become "friends" with a click of a button and then have the ability to see, comment, and even argue with each other. But throughout history, relationships took effort and time. The ability to speak into the lives of others was earned. This is the "social" media paradox. The founder and CEO of Social Media HQ, Christian Zilles, reflects: "In short, social media has fundamentally changed the way we think about relationships by speeding up the process of forming these relationships in the first place and then dramatically lowering the bar as to what it means to be in a relationship."[5]

As the bar is lowered, we can have more friends and connections around the world on various platforms; however, are we losing the ability to form deeper, meaningful friendships where we are known and loved and experience true belonging. I remember in the early days of email, I sent a message to break up with my ex-girlfriend because I didn't want to deal with my anxiety of having that painful conversation in person. (I'm sorry, former girlfriend!) Today, we have the option of "blocking" a person. Or just ghosting someone completely. This affects our ability to navigate relationships and eventually breaks down the quality of true friendship and community.

One quick note: we should not feel guilty for having acquaintances. Stanford sociology professor Mark Granovetter in his landmark study introduced the importance of these "weak-ties"[6] and why they matter—they help with searching for jobs and opportunities, gathering and learning new information, and engaging in lighter and less taxing conversations. These more casual relationships can be beneficial. But what I'm most concerned with is our inability to forge deep, meaningful belonging with others.

Phones and emails were designed for faster communication and connection but have now become a main source of distraction. I recently spent an hour during lunch with a pastor so that we could get to know each other. However, the pastor didn't ask any questions about my life. He talked the whole time, continually looked at his watch and phone, and could not maintain eye contact. He was constantly distracted and I left the lunch feeling even more disconnected. One of the key tasks for pastors is to shepherd God's people by listening and caring for the flock. This requires curiosity and active listening. The contrast in that meeting could not have been more stark.

Recent global data on emotional intelligence shows a steady decline. According to a 2018 report surveying more than 200,000 people across 160 countries, since 2011 there has been a steady decline of emotional intelligence by about 5 percent every year![7] Basic human communication skills are becoming hard to find. Though 2018 had better results in emotional intelligence for the first time, we've got a long way to go, and the global isolation in 2020 didn't help. Increased stress and anxiety levels, our current mental health crisis, infrequent face-to-face interactions, and more have had an impact on our emotional and social skills that are so crucial to interpersonal relationships. It affects our ability to deeply connect and experience a sense of belonging with others.

But let me pause and say this: technology can be a helpful tool as long as we are aware of its role in our lives. There is nothing wrong with catching up with a friend who lives three thousand miles away. My good friend Jay, the author of *Analog Church*, talks about how helpful technology is when traveling out of town. It's a wonderful gift to see his kids' faces while he talks with them on FaceTime, but it certainly does not replace holding and kissing them in real life. Author Andy Crouch reminds us, "Technology is in its proper place when it helps us bond with the real people we have been given to love. It's out of its proper place when we end up bonding with people at a distance, like celebrities, whom we will never meet."[8]

Sometimes, in this False Connection Cycle, we turn to things that keep us numb, like drugs and alcohol, and they literally become our false friends. In Korea, the hashtag #alcoholismyfriend (#술은내친구) had 31.7 million hits on Google.[9] Those Koreans say alcohol is a fantastic friend because it always listens, never corrects you, and is there for you no matter what. This hashtag proclaiming that alcohol is a friend is partially a joke, but the underlying truth is that alcohol is clearly used as a substitute for real human connection. It's easier to have a drink than to have a real talk. Or some rely on alcohol in their systems in order to be "real" with people.

Maybe we don't treat alcohol like our friend, but instead keep a regular date night with Netflix, vegging out through hours of streaming entertainment. Media addiction is indeed rampant. Researchers estimate that more than 210 million people suffer from it.[10] Certainly, we can say we are resting, and, yes, we do need breaks from our busy lives. But there is a difference between *self-care* and *self-soothe*. Self-soothe focuses more on feeling good at the moment, while self-care is being mindful of your needs and building long-term solutions. Self-care is eating well, working out, sleeping, taking walks, and watching your favorite shows. How could you go wrong with Korean fried chicken and rom-coms after a long day? But sometimes those necessary breaks simply become a way to numb ourselves to the world. This keeps us stuck in the False Connection Cycle.

For some, the temptation is the opposite of a Netflix binge: a never-ending workweek. I live in Silicon Valley, a place where work can be a kind of drug and being busy can be a badge of honor. Of course, workaholics are everywhere, not only in the land of work-all-night start-ups. Work can be a means to avoiding the pain of loneliness by staying busy and pouring all our energy into our work, hoping that our performance, achievements, and success will offer us the belonging and fulfillment we are looking for.

In desperate situations, the pursuit of inappropriate relationships can be a destructive false connection. We begin these "innocent" conversations in our search connection where it quickly escalates to temporarily satisfy our sexual or emotional needs that are outside the bounds in our commitments whether it be our workplace, marriage, society, or faith community.

Maybe you can't relate because you're an independent, strong, self-sufficient type of person. In my friend group and at work, I often hear "I'm not lonely, I'm fine!" But I wonder if inside, they may be hoping someone will see beyond their wall and love them for who they are.

Most of us habitually turn to one of these false connections to distract ourselves and temporarily forget our painful inner loneliness, whether we are aware of it or not, and these things can leave us less whole, less connected, and less human.

All of this substituting leads to the third step in the False Connection Cycle: *feeling anxious and lonely from lack of real intimacy and belonging.* If we don't deal with the source of these symptoms, we can experience further destruction emotionally, spiritually, and physically. We can experience long periods of despair, self-hatred, and other forms of self-harm. We can say to ourselves, *No one gets me. No one really cares. I'm all by myself.*

Though our culture and society are connected more than ever (via Facebook, Instagram, email, texts, ease of travel), 61 percent of Americans feel lonely.[11] Our basic human need for community isn't being met. But we should expect different results for Christians, right?

In my own research of more than thirteen hundred people of diverse demographics (age, sex, and ethnicity) who consider themselves Christians, I found that when asked, "What are you currently struggling with?"[12] an overwhelming majority of the participants responded, "Loneliness."

And this research was done a year *before* the COVID-19 pandemic.

Furthermore, of these respondents, half were actively participating in various church groups—small groups, recovery groups, Bible studies, and community groups. Anxiety, stress, false connections, and loneliness among Christians are still nearly identical to the national statistics, despite the opportunities to connect at church.

So what's really happening here?

AN HONEST LOOK AT CHRISTIAN COMMUNITY

Before we move on, let me remind you, I am a pastor. I believe in the local church. I believe that the Christian community offers us a new family in Christ, a place of real belonging. But we are here to have an honest evaluation of Christian community, remember? If you are a church leader like me, this is going to hurt a bit, but hopefully, this will be a helpful catalyst as we think pastorally and strategically about our people.

I spend most of my time finding ways to help people connect and find their next step in our community. To help them deal with the issues they struggle with. To find community. And yet, in my experience, while churches promise real connection and belonging, in reality, it looks more like this:

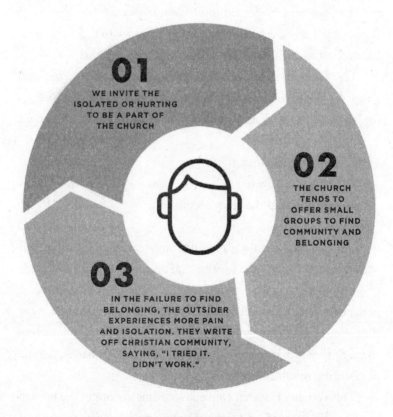

01

WE INVITE THE ISOLATED OR HURTING TO BE A PART OF THE CHURCH

02

THE CHURCH TENDS TO OFFER SMALL GROUPS TO FIND COMMUNITY AND BELONGING

03

IN THE FAILURE TO FIND BELONGING, THE OUTSIDER EXPERIENCES MORE PAIN AND ISOLATION. THEY WRITE OFF CHRISTIAN COMMUNITY, SAYING, "I TRIED IT. DIDN'T WORK."

THE UNINTENTIONAL CHURCH CYCLE

I call this the Unintentional Church Cycle because this collapse in community is not what any church wants, but it is sadly an all-too-common experience.

The first step begins when *the Christian community invites the isolated or hurt person to be part of the church.* Nowadays, churches regularly use the phrase "You Belong Here" or "We Are Family" on social media, flyers, and websites. It's a beautiful invitation that stems from the gospel story that we were all once orphans, living in our own ways without Christ, and through His life, death, and resurrection, we are adopted into belonging in the family of God (Ephesians 1:3–8). As we have received, we work to share the same connection with everyone who walks into our churches.

This leads us to the second step: *the church tends to offer small groups for folks seeking community and belonging.* Specifically, *belonging* is often nicely packaged into the church's formula for connection:

1. Join a small group
2. Serve in a ministry
3. Rally around the church's mission

This process of joining a small group, serving in ministry, and connecting to the broader mission and vision of the church sounds good in theory—great, in fact. But, there is no such thing as a perfect system that produces and guarantees perfect results every time. Some folks do experience meaningful belonging by moving through these rhythms of church life. But, unfortunately, despite our best intentions, some folks do not.

This system of church connection primarily places the burden on the individual to find a sense of belonging—but what happens if they don't? If they don't experience the belonging they were hoping for and that was promised, they leave believing it is their fault for not properly working through the system.

Of course, belonging does call for some individual responsibility. Actually, that's what most of this book is about. But the research shows that Christian community has not thought deeply about how their spaces of belonging operate, and how effective they are in truly bringing about belonging by welcoming all.

So, we arrive at the last step of the cycle: *in the failure to find belonging, the outsider experiences only more pain and isolation.* They write off Christian community, saying, "I tried it. Didn't work."

Side by side, the data nationally and within Christian communities is the same: we're drowning in loneliness and anxiety. Friends, we have a *crisis of belonging.* But let me share with you why I believe there's a reason for great hope.

I CAN'T CARRY IT,
BUT I CAN CARRY YOU

I rarely watch the same movie twice, and if I do, it has to be one of the best. *Braveheart. Titanic.* (Yes, I said *Titanic.*[13]) But near the top of that short list for me is the Lord of the Rings trilogy. If you've seen it, you'll recall this epic scene in *The Return of the King*:

Toward the end of Frodo's quest to Mount Doom to throw the evil ring into the fire, his faithful friend Samwise takes the fallen Frodo in his arms and reminds him of their shared memories of their home. Fighting the darkness and fear, Samwise summons his last bit of strength and says, "Come on, Mr. Frodo! I can't carry it for you, but I can carry you!"

Popular wisdom would say that to know a Sam, we have to be a

Sam. But how can we be like Samwise? One day as I was rewatching this scene and pondering this, Tolkien's words pulled my heart to recognize what I'd been missing. This is what we really want. We *all* long for this kind of friendship and community. Someone like Samwise to come alongside us in our despair and confusion, to see our fears and loneliness, and offer such tenacious hope and tangible help. Someone who shows up for us, even if we cannot show up for ourselves.

Our ancient wisdom literature in the Bible, which is about life's good gifts from God, mentions this beauty of belonging and friendship as well:

> Two are better than one, because they have a good reward for their toil. For if they fall, one will lift up his fellow. But woe to him who is alone when he falls and has not another to lift him up! Again, if two lie together, they keep warm, but how can one keep warm alone? And though a man might prevail against one who is alone, two will withstand him—a threefold cord is not quickly broken. (Ecclesiastes 4:9–12)

These verses paint a picture of what we truly want. We are all tired of false connections that leave us dissatisfied. We long for deeper spiritual and relational connections, real soul-friends. And something in us senses we can only experience true belonging, intimacy, and transformation when our whole selves become fully known and loved. But that kind of connection is so hard in this digital age, where we have access to tools that continuously use filters to beautify, cover up, and add false constructs we want to portray about ourselves. A diversity of genders, ethnicities, ages, and cultures brings additional challenges to belonging. While

God has given us the gift of family, friends, neighbors, coworkers, Christian community, and small groups, finding *real* belonging is still a very difficult matter for many people.

FIVE PRACTICES FOR BELONGING

The good news is that we *all* want to belong—we simply don't know how. And maybe we fear having to go through something like Frodo and Sam did to get there. It's become one of my life's missions to find out how belonging works, largely because this has been my own journey. I needed to find these answers for myself. In my research, I uncovered what I believe are the five practices for creating a meaningful and transformative community:

> Practice #1: **PRIORITY**—Let's Talk About Our Commitment Issues
>
> Practice #2: **CHEMISTRY**—The Difference Between *Clique* and *Click*
>
> Practice #3: **VULNERABILITY**—Lowering the Wall of Shame for Connection
>
> Practice #4: **EMPATHY**—Supporting Others Well in a Self-Absorbed World
>
> Practice #5: **ACCOUNTABILITY**—The Necessary Road to Christlikeness

No matter who you are or where you are in this journey, these five are the essential tools to unlock our diverse selves and be fully known and loved. I will walk with you through each one so you can see how it helps us create true belonging.

But before we begin, I have one question for you:

What has your journey of belonging been like and where is it headed?

There's a fascinating story in Genesis 16 about Abram, Sarai, and Hagar. Abram and Sarai, as followers of Yahweh, were supposed to be the very community that protected and cared for individuals like Hagar, who was an outsider. But instead of receiving belonging, Hagar was mistreated and abused. Abram and Sarai didn't even call her by name. Hagar then fled from them, desperately seeking her own way, but the angel of the Lord found her and asked this incredible question: "Where have you come from and where are you going?" (Genesis 16:8).

The entire story of the Bible is about God—a pursuing God, a consistent God, a relentless God. I love that when Hagar wasn't even looking for God, God was looking for her. This is the entire story of the Bible. God is pursuing people, even when they don't know it.

God certainly knows where we have come from and where we are going. But He asked Hagar and is ultimately asking us: *Where have you come from and where are you going?*

I'd like to invite you to self-reflect. Think through your childhood, family relationships, friends, workplaces, Christian communities. All of it. The good, the bad, and the ugly. What are some of the disappointing and painful experiences you are carrying and running away from in your history of belonging? And when you've considered some of the most significant experiences there, what false connections have you used to cope with your loneliness? Where are you seeking belonging? And where might God be seeking you in order to connect?

This is obviously an ongoing journey, like Frodo's, with new layers of discovery. Don't get overwhelmed with too much of that now. We'll work through those together in this book.

For now, let's explore how our ability to belong was largely determined by where we all started: our childhood.

Chapter 2

Barriers to Belonging

I sat in my kitchen, staring at the unopened letter.

It was spring of my senior year in high school, and after sending out applications to many colleges, I was starting to hear back from them. Including this one.

My dream college. My number one choice. My first love.

I had worked *so hard* to get into this school. I had played four years of volleyball all because I thought it would make me look more well-rounded as an admissions applicant. I think I played a grand total of four minutes in my entire volleyball career. I was so mediocre that the team actually forgot about me during the yearbook photo. But I didn't care. The only thing that mattered to me was getting to my dream college.

I was excited and nauseous all at the same time, like how I felt when I tried to talk to girls. My parents weren't home yet, but I wasn't going to wait for them. If I got in, I'd have a heck of a surprise for them. If I didn't get in, I'd have a few hours to hide the evidence. With my shaking hands, I finally opened the letter. It read:

Thank you for your interest in our program but we regret that we cannot offer you admission at this time. We have received an amazing pool of applicants with strong accomplishments but due to our limited space, we were only able to accept a few.

What?

I was stunned.

It took several moments for the words to register. And as I sat in the kitchen, I felt my hope of belonging to this new community die within me. I'd dreamed of buying my parents hoodies and car stickers with the school's name as a reminder to them and everyone else that we belonged there.

I thought about all the SAT prep classes I'd taken. About all the time I'd spent learning vocabulary words so that I could do better on the analogy portion of the test. I thought about all the hours I spent doing extracurricular activities to impress potential colleges that I didn't even care about.

I thought about how my family had sacrificed so much time and money for this moment. I thought about how my mom would now have to face the other Korean mothers at local coffee shops and in our church's fellowship hall and would have to answer the question, "So, did David get into his number one choice school?" And she would have to say, "No. He's a failure." (At least that is what I believed they would hear.)

At the end of my eighth grade year, our family had moved to a new town twenty minutes farther from my dad's work for one reason—to allow me to attend a better school that would give me a better shot at getting into my dream college.

Now it was all gone. I hadn't gotten in. I was rejected.

My dream college had rejected me.[1]

I share all this because I still remember that moment. Trauma has a weird way of sticking with us. And in that moment, in my kitchen, a toxic and deeply held belief about belonging was reinforced inside me: Belonging happens only when you are worthy of belonging. Therefore, the only way to prove to others I belong is through achievements and success. It didn't help that this thinking was reinforced by religious, cultural, and societal values. Stereotypes such as the Model Minority Myth made me believe staying quiet, educated, and successful was the way to belong and differentiate from "problem minorities." So I had put my head down, worked hard, and tried never to rock the boat.

How many of us went through the pain of waiting to be picked in a team game? Or of being passed over on an invite to a party or work event? We say to ourselves, "Maybe I'm not _____ enough," and even if it makes sense, there's grief and even despair involved in not belonging.

DOING AS BELONGING

This belief also exists in Christian communities: if I can correctly perform and do what is expected of me, then my seat at the table won't be taken away from me.

Many of us were taught in the Christian community to:
first, *behave*,
then, *believe*,
and finally, *belong*.

As a result, we spend our lives trying to fit in, behaving in the "right way" to be accepted, to belong. We try to present a perfect version of ourselves. We practice virtue-signaling, hoping someone will notice our "good works" and see us as more mature and put together. And in the process, we abandon ourselves in order to be what others want us to be. It's exhausting. We think we belong but it's a fragile, false version. Why? Because it's not the real you and me. It's a made-up version of ourselves.

This is understandable. For many, if we show our honest selves, we are met with harshness and disrespect. Or we are plainly ignored. The hurt results in distancing ourselves from Christian communities. And these experiences cause us to believe lies about who we are and how belonging works, even our belonging with God. We begin to believe that our good works and good behavior are requirements for belonging to Jesus. So we work hard to make sure we are worth keeping around. Friends, that is not the gospel of good news. It's terrible news.

NEUROSCIENCE AND THE NERVOUS SYSTEM

We all carry our own history of acceptance and rejection in our search for belonging. We are now learning from neuroscience that our brains are plastic. Not literally plastic but rather that they are moldable and can physically change as a result of experience.

Bessel van der Kolk, in his book *The Body Keeps the Score*, says,

> We have learned that trauma is not just an event that took place sometime in the past; it is also the imprint left by that experience on mind, brain, and body. This imprint has ongoing consequences for how the human organism manages to survive in the present.

Trauma results in a fundamental reorganization of the way mind and brain manage perceptions. It changes not only how we think and what we think about, but also our very capacity to think.[2]

Our body's command center—called the nervous system—may automatically trigger a response of fight, flight, freeze, or fawn if our bodies perceive a threat. These physiological and psychological reactions are often involuntary. They are designed for self-protection and are learned through experiences, both good and bad. This is why someone who previously had a poor experience with an authority figure might feel his body tense when an authority figure enters the room.

It's also why we might shut down with certain people, or why we tend to pick fights as someone tries to get close. Or we may become so desperate and needy that it causes folks to avoid us altogether. Our bodies actually store trauma and send us into a certain posture as we try to move into belonging. It impacts how we think, react, and relate to others. To put it another way, we all have *dysfunctional approaches to belonging*, and there is healing to be found in recognizing what ours are.

Jesus followers know that all human dysfunctions are ultimately tied to sin. This is what sin does: stains, corrupts, twists, and destroys everything good in this world. In the words of David Taylor, anything that depletes, diminishes, or corrupts life is like a death.[3] Sin, as we read in the earliest pages of the Bible, brings separation in all forms of relationships, with God and others. Sin affects our belonging, the way we connect and love one another. By the way, sin isn't just something that we do. Sin can be something that is also done to us. Sin brings much pain and ultimately death. In the words of the apostle Paul to the Corinthian church, "The sting of death is sin, and the power of sin is the law" (1 Corinthians 15:56).

Before you get discouraged, wait for his next words: "But thanks be to God, who gives us the victory through our Lord Jesus Christ" (v. 57). Jesus came to defeat sin and death and will come again to bring full healing and restoration to all that was lost. And with His power, we as His children face sin and brokenness not with despair but with strength and courage.

So I share these dysfunctions not as hopeless diagnoses but as ways to invite the Spirit to work within us. Not knowing the dysfunctions that cause barriers to our belonging is like getting a sports massage from someone who hasn't diagnosed where you are tight or injured. While the massage may be helpful, focusing on where you are hurting actually accelerates the healing and makes it more effective.

So what are the four dysfunctions anyway?

THE FOUR DYSFUNCTIONS

All our experiences of belonging, from childhood to now, shape how we think about relationships and our posture toward them. If we are not aware of how we pursue belonging with others (or don't), we will find ourselves sabotaging the very thing we want.

When we seek belonging, each of us has a particular way we relate to others in what I call the four dysfunctions. They are:

Avoidant
Anxious

Aggressive

Accommodating

When you join a community or engage in a conversation with someone, people will often experience you in one of these ways. Therefore, it's important to be aware of your belonging tendency and how it affects you and others. I wish I'd known mine earlier in my journey. For many years, I struggled to understand why it was so hard for me to keep meaningful relationships.

Because many of our belonging tendencies are done subconsciously, it takes work to identify them, but if we can recognize our patterns and develop healthier ways to interact and respond, it can be a game changer in our belonging journey.

As you read these, which one seems true of you? What tends to be your default?

Avoidant

You are walled off. You believe you can survive on your own and/or think that others are not worthy to belong with you. You need your space, so you avoid people and conversations that will drain your energy. You secretly ask yourself: *Do I really need others and is pursuing belonging worth my time and energy?*

My wife, Nina, graciously gave me permission to name her here. In the family she grew up in, no one asked about her personal needs and concerns. They left her alone, and while she enjoyed the freedom and space, she didn't realize how much she needed care. She became conditioned to be alone, and in any setting with people, including our family, she still consistently desires alone time.

Anxious

There is an overwhelming amount of fear and caution in your approach to relationships. It's hard to trust others and there is a ton of shame so that often you withdraw from others. You secretly ask yourself: *Will others truly accept me, and will it be okay for me to belong here?*

A friend of mine shared with me that she has been betrayed by the very people who were supposed to protect and nurture her. This causes her to be suspicious and skeptical in approaching any new relationship.

Aggressive

You move toward others out of pride and strength. You believe you should choose who belongs in your circle. You frequently sabotage relationships due to control and anger. You secretly ask yourself: *Can I be weak and still belong?*

My buddy Josh grew up in a foster care system where much was taken from him. At one home, he was living with fifteen other children, so he had to seize control and fight for himself to eat and even shower with clean water. Today, he has a hard time trusting anyone and keeps himself very private. His aggression comes from self-protection and testing who can handle his energy.

Accommodating

You love to please others. Due to your neediness in relationships, you seek attention and/or approval from others. You change and adapt who you are so that you can be whoever others want you to be. You secretly ask yourself: *What do they want me to be, and what can I do to belong?*

Dave, another dear friend, shared that one of his classmates once asked him, "What was wrong with you that your mom wanted to get rid of you?" Dave had been adopted, and the question haunted him. He coped by becoming a class clown to receive more attention, love, and acceptance. Today, he no longer views himself as an unwanted child who was adopted, but he still loves to be helpful, a trait that he developed to fend off feelings of being unwanted, unneeded, discarded.

CASE STUDY

Genesis 16 captures an interesting relational dynamic between Abram, Sarai, and Hagar. As you read the account below, try to identify which dysfunction (avoidant, anxious, aggressive, or accommodating) you see for each person as they navigate their journey of belonging.

> Now Sarai, Abram's wife, had borne him no children. But she had an Egyptian slave named Hagar; so she said to Abram, "The LORD has kept me from having children. Go, sleep with my slave; perhaps I can build a family through her."
>
> Abram agreed to what Sarai said. So after Abram had been living in Canaan ten years, Sarai his wife took her Egyptian slave Hagar and gave her to her husband to be his wife. He slept with Hagar, and she conceived.

When she knew she was pregnant, she began to despise her mistress. Then Sarai said to Abram, "You are responsible for the wrong I am suffering. I put my slave in your arms, and now that she knows she is pregnant, she despises me. May the LORD judge between you and me."

"Your slave is in your hands," Abram said. "Do with her whatever you think best." Then Sarai mistreated Hagar; so she fled from her.

The angel of the LORD found Hagar near a spring in the desert; it was the spring that is beside the road to Shur. And he said, "Hagar, slave of Sarai, where have you come from, and where are you going?"

"I'm running away from my mistress Sarai," she answered.

(GENESIS 16:1–8 NIV)

You may have noticed that Sarai's aggressive posture is very obvious. Since she couldn't bear a child, she tried to build a family by encouraging her husband, Abram, to sleep with her slave, Hagar. Then, when he did, she blamed Abram for Hagar's pregnancy.

In response, Abram, our "father of faith," said to Sarai, "Your slave is in your hands . . . do with her whatever you think best" (v. 6 NIV). He avoided a difficult conversation with Sarai, and that accommodating posture ended up harming Hagar, who was supposed to be in his care.

For safety, Hagar ran away from this toxic family. Her avoidant posture is understandable and yet the angel of the Lord asked her to examine what she was really doing and strengthened her to face what she was avoiding all along. (Let me pause to emphasize that this story is not encouraging someone who is being abused to go back to abusers or toxic environments.)

Perhaps you've noticed that each of these four dysfunctions are more or less motivated by some kind of fear, and each is a crippling or destructive way to interact with others. However, as we find healing, there is another way to live in our journey of belonging. Instead of living in our dysfunctions, we can move toward what I call an *anchored* way.

Anchored

You are both calm and confident in who you are. While there is an openness and humility toward relationships, at the same time, you have strong boundaries and wisdom in navigating what's healthy and what's toxic. You say to yourself this truth: *I am created to belong and I need others.*

The first part of that statement is a reminder of our worth. The Bible says that we are made in the image of God (Genesis 1:27). We are fearfully and wonderfully made because He carefully knit us in our mother's womb (Psalm 139:14–16). My friend Ben said it like this: "God didn't just open the cosmic refrigerator and make us with all the leftovers inside the fridge. He uniquely made each one of us with His best stuff . . . fine cheese, choice cuts of meat, and sourdough!"

No matter where you are in your belonging journey, this is where we long to be. When we say yes to Jesus' invitation of forgiveness and new life with Him, this anchor is unquestionably strong. Actually, it's unbreakable. Such worth knows that no matter what happens in our lives, we belong to Jesus (Romans 1:6) and nothing will be able to separate us from the love of God that is in Christ Jesus our Lord (Romans 8:39). The Holy Spirit takes up residence in our hearts, dwelling in us (1 Corinthians 6:19). We must not believe the lie that we are all alone, no one loves us, and we are not worth others' effort, all of which will eventually lead to self-rejection and self-hatred. We are designed by God to love and be loved. And we find our true belonging and home in the very loving presence of our triune God.

In the story of Abram, Sarai, and Hagar, Hagar was a non-Israelite slave living in a culture where she was ignored and treated as a lower-class citizen, yet she deeply understood that God is not distant, absent, or careless. Even though she was rejected by everyone and did not experience true belonging anywhere, including in the household of Abram, she knew that God saw her. She knew God cared about the innermost parts of her. God knows. So she responded with these words: "'You are the God who sees me,' for she said, 'I have now seen the One who sees me'" (Genesis 16:13 NIV). As with Hagar, God also sees us and calls all of us to remain and abide in His love daily.

This second part of that statement is a reminder of our frailty. We *do* need others. The Bible says, "In Christ, we, though many, form one body, and each member *belongs* to all the others" (Romans 12:5 NIV, emphasis added). We must not believe the lie that we can do this life alone. In his letter to the church in Corinth, Paul skillfully articulated the body principle for our interdependence: "The eye cannot say to the hand, 'I don't need you!' And the head cannot say to the feet, 'I don't need you!' On the contrary, those parts of the body that seem to be weaker are indispensable, and the parts that we think are less honorable we treat with special honor" (1 Corinthians 12:21–23 NIV). It would be silly for us to say we don't need some parts of our body. This is a profound truth worth pondering that we are designed by God to belong to one another for our flourishing.

The goal is to hold and anchor ourselves in both parts of this truth statement at the same time—worthiness and frailty. Holding only half will result in either arrogance or neediness. It is not easy to perfectly balance these, but it is possible with God's help to avoid both traps. Belonging, then, is first and foremost an inner work and reality.

Jesus modeled this *anchored* posture for us. In Matthew 4, the devil challenged Jesus' identity. He tempted Jesus by challenging Him to prove Himself if He really was the Son of God. But Jesus did not waver. He knew who He was and did not need to prove His worth or value. His Father's very words before Jesus even began His ministry, before saving the world by dying on the cross and resurrecting from the grave, "This is my beloved Son, with whom I am well pleased," became His anchor.

Jesus was also aware of His frailty and didn't do life alone. He later asked His disciples for their support and prayers: "And He took with Him Peter and the two sons of Zebedee, and He began to be sorrowful and deeply distressed. Then He said to them, 'My soul is very sorrowful, even to death; remain here, and watch with me'" (Matthew 26:37–38).

It's important to be self-aware and know what you bring to others in your journey of belonging. Are you avoidant, anxious, aggressive, or accommodating? I resonate most with the avoidant tendency. When I'm tired or busy, it's my default.

Even as I wrote this chapter, my four-year-old daughter, Zoey, tapped my shoulder. "Daddy, play with me." I felt myself going into the avoidant tendency that very moment.

From past experience, I created a belief that my time, resources, and energy were more important than anyone around me. And only with many kind invitations from Jesus have I begun to see underneath my walled-off posture and the reasons I didn't let anyone in.

How about you?

FROM OUR MOTHER'S WOMB

Our experiences with belonging shape us. From how our friends treated us on the playground to our history in the Christian community, every early experience teaches us what it means to belong, individually and in the community around us. Dr. Daniel Siegel, clinical professor of psychiatry at UCLA School of Medicine and author of *New York Times* bestseller *The Whole-Brain Child*, said,

> As children develop, their brains "mirror" their parent's brain.
> In other words, the parent's own growth and development, or
> lack of those, impact the child's brain. As parents become more
> aware and emotionally healthy, their children reap the rewards
> and move toward health as well.[4]

As babies, we come to the world looking for comfort, and studies have shown that "infants deprived of touch become lonely, isolated, and troublesome children."[5] Psychologist Abraham Maslow in his well-known Hierarchy of Needs put belonging and love right after food and shelter. I argue that belonging is as equally important to our survival and well-being as food and shelter. We need belonging to survive—certainly to thrive. And as children, we depend on our parents or guardians to provide it.

Milan and Kay Yerkovich, marriage counselors and authors of the bestselling book *How We Love*, explain it like this: "God designed us to need connection, and our relationships with our parents is the first place this happens—or doesn't happen."[6] In other words, whether we like it or not, our sense of belonging is deeply tied to our experience at home. It's where we spend most of our time observing, learning, and experiencing what it means to belong.

John Bowlby, the first attachment theorist, said that people's early relationships with their parents and/or caregivers are the foundation for how they will respond to others in relationships for the rest of their lives.[7] We learn intimacy from our parents.

My own parents are amazing. My dad has always been a fun-loving, caring, emotionally expressive man. He loves Jesus and models it. If I had one word to describe him, it would be *integrity*. My mom? She's also warm, caring, and silly. One word to describe her would be *sacrificial*. I am absolutely certain I would not be here today if it wasn't for her prayers.

My parents came to America trusting in God's call and provision like Abraham and Sarah. We didn't have much, but they did their best to provide and care for us with all the knowledge and resources they had at the time. They have given their entire lives in seeking first His kingdom and are my heroes of faith.

But like every family, we had struggles and pain. And like many pastors' homes, the bar was set high. Things had to be done

right.
godly.
perfect.

I felt that my every move was being watched.

My father was incredibly busy with ministry. He worked up to eighteen hours a day and beyond. He would frequently sleep in the church, too tired to drive home. The limited times he was available, though, he gave me all of his attention. I knew I was loved by both my parents, but my mom was the general of the house. She was busy executing the daily rhythms for all of us, and things were certainly tense at times.

This led me to believe my belonging in Christian community depended on my ability to achieve and maintain spiritual maturity. Not surprisingly, as an adult I also became busy with ministry; however, I didn't value deep, meaningful relationships. I focused more on the external preaching, events, and programs, measuring ministerial success strictly in numbers, and furthering my own education. I didn't know how to be vulnerable and open and I didn't believe anyone would want to know my failures. I was determined not to disappoint everyone's high expectations of me, so without knowing it, I became *avoidant* when people got too close. I put up a wall they could not climb. And in this way, I believed that my time, energy, and resources were more important than anyone and anything else. In trying to protect myself, I became selfish and self-centered.

After looking at my past and the dysfunctions I'd developed, I have become better equipped to create healthy belonging. I encourage you to do the same by answering these questions:

What was your home experience like growing up?
When you were distressed and needed comfort, how did your
parents generally respond?

I remember my girls at birth, crying and pooping everywhere (mostly on my wife). But we embraced them with such joy and gratitude. We loved them so much. Why? Because they accomplished something for us? Of course not! Our love was pure and unconditional.

Babies are born into belonging. They don't have to earn it; they have nothing to prove. They are beloved *before* they accomplish anything. And they thrive best in the confidence of that secure place.

Somehow, we adults have lost our way.

WHOSE FAULT IS IT ANYWAY?

Conversations about our upbringing can go in a few different directions. If you come from an honor and shame culture like mine, you may feel it is sinful to process your parents' shortcomings. Christians also know the Bible says to honor your father and mother (Exodus 20:12). We may want to cover their "shame," like in the story of Noah and his sons in Genesis 9. Our individualistic culture may contribute to this resistance as well. We may think, *How are my caregivers relevant to my journey of belonging?*

To make this even more complex, our sin nature and difficulties in belonging tend to make us blame others. We can even target Christian communities as the sole reason for our struggle. And then we move from community to community, blaming each for our lack of connection. My pastor Steve said, "When Bob has a problem with Jon, and Bob has a problem with Nicole, and Bob has a problem with Andy, who has the real problem?"

We can't blame our parents or others for our problems. But in trying to understand how we have been shaped, and to learn better ways to belong, moving forward means first looking back.

Blaming and not taking responsibility is part of our human story dating back to Genesis 3. When God spoke to Adam and Eve after they had taken the fruit, Adam blamed both God and Eve for his problem. "*The woman* whom *You* gave to be with me, she gave me [fruit] of the tree." Eve then blamed "*the serpent* [who] deceived me" (vv. 12–13 NKJV, emphasis added).

We are no different when we complain or cast blame or when our thoughts sound similar to these:

It's their fault!

They have no warmth and openness!
I'm treated as an outsider!
They are too clique-y!

Certainly, these could be true, but they also could be indicative of something more serious and damaging. There might be some work to be done on our end as well.

What would our lives look like if we took responsibility and uncovered the work we need to do in order to experience meaningful connection and belonging? We'd need some powerful self-awareness tools to begin the work, specifically the kind that honestly examines ourselves, neither blaming our parents nor ignoring how our experiences have affected us.[8]

Unfortunately, when the subject of self-awareness comes up, some Christians become uncomfortable. The word brings up thoughts of "New Age spirituality" or "self-help" or seems too me-centered and not enough Jesus-and-others focused. But Luke records Jesus' teaching this way: "Why do you look at the speck of sawdust in your brother's eye and pay no attention to the plank in your own. . . . You hypocrite" (Luke 6:41–42 NIV).

Though spoken to the religious leaders, Jesus invited all of us to be self-aware and examine ourselves. Humans are prone to always point and see the problem in others, neglecting our own inner work. It's easier to judge and blame others than to face our own reality. This is why St. Teresa of Avila wrote, "Almost all problems in the spiritual life stem from lack of self-knowledge."[9] Therefore, our goal must be to invite God into all the parts of ourselves that we may not be even aware of, and by His grace, reveal to us our blind spots to receive healing and freedom. In the words of the psalmist, we pray, "Search me, God, and know my heart; test me and know my anxious thoughts. See if there is any offensive way in me, and lead me in the way everlasting" (Psalm 139:23–24 NIV).

Understanding who we are and who we are not is essential to how we engage with others and even to our journey with God (Romans 12:3). John the Baptist had clarity about his own identity. When faced with the question, "Who are you and what do you say about yourself?" he responded, "I am not the Christ, Elijah, or the Prophet. But I am the voice of one calling in the wilderness" (John 1:19–23, author paraphrase). Do we have this kind of clarity about ourselves?

Belonging is tough, but it is possible, especially if we address our dysfunctional belonging tendencies that work against the Five Practices for cultivating community. We've discussed how our default belonging tendency comes from our childhood and key relational experiences in our lives, fused with cultural, societal, and religious values growing up. But we've also learned that we can unlearn through practicing healthy elements of belonging.

The first step in our journey of belonging is being responsible for how we engage our own stories. We will then understand why we default to a certain belonging tendency.

As you reflect, you may want to say a prayer that I've used:

Jesus, I am mindful that my default belonging tendency is one of avoidance. I long to belong, but I believe in the lie that I can do this life alone. If I'm being honest, I'm covering my insecurity with pride. I am deeply insecure about my worth. I need Your healing grace to touch my belief that stems all the way from my childhood that belonging happens when I am worthy of belonging. I need You, Jesus.

I also recommend taking some time to work through the following section. Once you do, you are ready to explore the Five Practices, which I believe will challenge and stretch you (as they have me) toward genuine community and belonging.

Barriers to Belonging Reflection

The great reformer John Calvin said, "Our wisdom consists almost entirely of two parts: knowledge of God and of ourselves." And in the words of Dr. Henry Cloud, "He [Jesus] is the Truth, and He wants us to deal in truth with ourselves and our loved ones. We want the truth about you and your family to flood into and overrun the secrets that keep you in bondage to dysfunctional behavior and relationships."[10] Let's take an honest inventory of ourselves with God's help.

What is your primary belonging tendency? Could you explore how each experience below has contributed to that particular dysfunction?

- Relationship with caregivers growing up
- Family values and upbringings
- Cultural and societal values
- Religious settings
- Past and present wounds

What prayer could you say, asking Jesus to help you overcome that dysfunction?

Part Two

HOW BELONGING IS POSSIBLE

Learning to forge meaningful relationships and experience healthy belonging in community can feel daunting, especially when we've had dysfunctional tendencies in relating. Where do we start? In my research, I uncovered what I believe are the best ways to create deep connection and belonging that are based on biblical wisdom.

THE FIVE PRACTICES

Practice #1: **PRIORITY**—Let's Talk About Our Commitment Issues

Practice #2: **CHEMISTRY**—The Difference Between *Clique* and *Click*

Practice #3: **VULNERABILITY**—Lowering the Wall of Shame for Connection

Practice #4: **EMPATHY**—Supporting Others Well in a Self-Absorbed World

Practice #5: **ACCOUNTABILITY**—The Necessary Road to Christlikeness

These core and foundational practices are designed to give weight and substance in our shallow world so that we don't drift away from what matters: connection.

Chapter 3

Practice #1: Priority

LET'S TALK ABOUT OUR COMMITMENT ISSUES

I s there any more disconnecting experience than the first day of school? When I came to America and began fifth grade, everything was foreign and I felt like an alien. Before I knew where I was supposed to sit for lunch, whether anyone would talk to me, or if I would be able to do the schoolwork, I had to face the toughest obstacle of all: increasing pressure on my bladder. I needed to use the restroom, but I didn't know how to ask.

As soon as the teacher walked in, she could tell I was lost. I didn't speak the language, I did not have friends, and everything around me felt strange. On the second day of school, she started class by announcing, "Today we are going to start with an activity. I'm handing out paper for each of you to pick some items to draw and write down what that item is in English."

Then she looked at me and said, "David, underneath the English word, I want you to write what that is in Korean." I knew what was happening. Though I didn't have the words for it yet, she was intentionally prioritizing my journey of belonging in America within the structure of the class and helping me identify and pronounce everything I would need to know in the classroom.

She did that for one new, unknown student.

Me.

But she didn't have to.

Immediately, I felt seen and known. I was a stranger on day one, but by day two, I had experienced belonging. I've moved more than twenty times in my life and I still have that binder with all the drawings and labels as a visible reminder of the power of prioritizing belonging.

LESSONS FROM THE DEATHBED

As a palliative nurse, Bronnie Ware spent countless hours supporting terminally ill patients in their final twelve weeks of life. In her bestselling memoir *The Top Five Regrets of the Dying*, Ware wrote that the top two regrets people have are:

I wish I had stayed in touch with my friends.
I wish I hadn't worked so hard.

We are constantly distracted, interrupted, and busy with this thing called life. In our cluttered and noisy world, we are bombarded with messages, texts, social media, and emails that often seem to be urgent. "Watch this thing." "Send this work email." "Join this program now." I live in Silicon Valley and people move here for work—not often for relationships. Many are here to chase after money, influence, fame, and career advancement. Bronnie Ware wrote:

> Often [the patients] would not truly realize the full benefits of old friends until their dying weeks and it was not always possible to track them down. Many had become so caught up in their own lives that they had let golden friendships slip by over the years. There were many deep regrets about not giving friendships the time and effort that they deserved. Everyone misses their friends when they are dying."[1]

I don't share this to shame you. Rather, these two regrets ring true for me personally. In my life's journey, I did not value and prioritize meaningful relationships. As a poor immigrant, I had other priorities, mainly to be educated and succeed here in America. I *had* to work hard, and eventually, I grew to love working a lot of hours. Today, those who are close to me know how terrible I am at keeping in touch. Even as a pastor, I easily can become selfish with my time, resources, and energy. This is why my priorities in life eventually got disordered.

Like many of us, I'm recovering from addiction to myself. Even as I juggle my work, ministry, and the deadline of this book, I need to stay deeply aware that I have the capability to ignore relationships altogether—the very thing I'm writing about! The struggle is real.

Priority is the first practice of belonging because it's what everything else stems from.

DESIGNED FOR DISCONNECTION

Dr. Kelly-Ann Allen is a senior lecturer and educational and developmental psychologist. She is a researcher on belonging, and in her article "Making Sense of Belonging,"[2] Allen reminds us that living alone wasn't an option for people during most of history. Instead, humans depended on belonging, living in groups, and cooperating with others for survival and safety. Today, though, many of us now have the "luxury" and the resources to live on our own. Before we take pride in our civilization's advancements, however, remember that this comfort comes at a high cost. It affects the way we live and interact with others and, ultimately, as Christ followers, the way we live out the teachings of Jesus in Christian community.

On this matter of choosing priorities, it's important to recognize that our society has dramatically changed, especially in the last ten years. Most of us have nearly unlimited access to more distractions than humans have ever encountered before. Through a smartphone, we have access to knowledge on any subject at the touch of our fingertips. When we are tempted to disengage from reality, we have a variety of entertainment options. Our natural curiosity and desire to dispel boredom makes our smartphone a priority by default. With endless clicks and scrolls, we can escape our present life even while actual humans are all around us.

Much of the West and many parts of the world have moved away from the tight-knit communities our grandparents experienced. The call for jobs, education, and regular travel has made it easier for us to uproot and go elsewhere. These pursuits that make us more transient aren't necessarily bad in themselves, but they can be dangerous in our journey of belonging if we aren't mindful. For example, there is a big difference between moving because we're restless, constantly chasing after the next big thing, and moving because our rent has become unaffordable.

Sebastian Junger, an award-winning journalist, once said, "The accumulation of personal property allowed people to make more and more individualistic choices about their lives. . . . A person living in a modern city or a suburb can, for the first time in history, go through an entire day—or an entire life—mostly encountering complete strangers. They can be surrounded by others and yet feel deeply, dangerously alone."[3] I would also add, we can go through an entire day without encountering *anyone*. And many people are opting for this. We can shop and gather information online, at the touch of a button. In either case, unless we now prioritize connecting with people in meaningful ways, the structure of our modern society is designed for disconnection. It leads us to actually believe we can live without others.

Before the entrance of rampant individualism, belonging provided safety and often easier access to fulfilling physiological needs in most societies.[4] In other words, going back to Maslow's Hierarchy of Needs and flipping the order, belonging to others in community actually had higher priority. Since we are able to meet our basic needs all by ourselves, the need for belonging has taken a back seat, and now we are paying for it with the pain of loneliness and high anxiety.

This is why it's so important to heed the warning and encouragement offered in the book of Hebrews. The author reminded us that living in difficult times calls for us to prioritize drawing near to Jesus and not to give up "meeting together, as some are in the *habit* of doing, but encouraging one another—and all the more as you see the Day approaching" (Hebrews 10:25 NIV, emphasis added). It is so easy for us to devalue our need for connection and habitually say, "Maybe later," or "When I feel like it and have more time." My habit is to be selfish with my time or withdraw from others when there is a conflict in a relationship. I have lost countless good friends because of that. What might be your pattern in relationships? We desperately need to fight to prioritize relationships. No matter where you are on the introvert-extrovert spectrum, whether it's easy or hard for you to start conversations with others, prioritizing will bring focus to your belonging journey.

"I HAVE A LEGITIMATE EXCUSE!"

I hear you. I understand that there might be some real reasons for not prioritizing belonging. You might be raising young children at home. You've already cleaned the house for the seventh time today and it's only 3:00 p.m. Life is crazy. You can't even remember what you had for dinner last night. Or you might be working multiple jobs to make ends meet for yourself or your family. There might be an illness in your family that requires a lot of attention. You don't have the time or the energy. I totally get that. Life is dynamic and complex, and these are all good and important things!

But isn't this when we need to lean into community all the more? We need help from those who deeply care about us. We need all of it: Prayers. Encouragement. Support. Understanding. Empathy. Care.

Notice how the author of Hebrews didn't say "keep meeting together unless you have young children, are tired, busy with work and life, going to graduate school, or have a knee problem." We need to do it all the more as we see "the Day [of Jesus' return] approaching."

In his compelling book *The Ruthless Elimination of Hurry*, John Mark Comer wrote: "Corrie ten Boom once said that if the devil can't make you sin, he'll make you busy. There's truth in that. Both sin and busyness have the exact same effect—they cut off your connection to God, to other people, and even to your own soul."[5] The devil will try to keep us from pursuing what's most important.

I often hear people say, "I've worked so hard in prioritizing relationships only to see them move out of town." Here in Silicon Valley this happens over and over again and people feel too defeated to try again. I also hear people say, "I've had disappointing experiences with people and Christian community. I don't want to get hurt again." While these responses are understandable, there's a saying by an unknown author that "some friends are for a reason, some are for a season, and some are for a lifetime." We have to check our expectations on friendships, but regardless, we need them and should pursue them.

157,680 HOURS

So what does it look like to *prioritize* belonging? Is it as simple as spending more time with those whom we would like to experience belonging? Adding up the time we spend with family and the hours we spend in the car, at meals, on vacations, and in daily conversations during our first eighteen years of life, we have lived 157,680 hours. If we lived at home during that time, we likely were in close proximity to family. That's a lot of hours—but many people have not experienced deep and meaningful belonging even within their families. While time and proximity are foundational and create more opportunities for deeper connection, they are not enough.

Belonging requires *intentionality*—in other words, prioritization. We cannot control others, so we need to be proactive about the relationships we want. In the early years of our marriage, my wife, Nina, would periodically remind me that her primary love language is quality time (though after becoming a mom of two girls, her primary love language seems to have changed to acts of service, which now brings *much* joy to her soul). Yet even from the beginning, she longed for intentional time that would foster greater intimacy and connection.

ACCIDENTAL VS. INTENTIONAL

Our relationship with Jesus is the same way. We may spend hours each week just going through the motions, mindlessly going in and out of prayer, Bible time, and church. We can be in the presence of Jesus without prioritizing Him in our minds and hearts.

I can't help but think of one of my favorite passages in the Bible: Luke 8. I've preached from this passage more than any other.

In those verses, Jesus was in Galilee. Having heard of His wisdom and power, large crowds had been following Him everywhere. His disciples were doing what they could to manage it, but it was quickly getting out of control. Imagine it being like the last big concert or sports game you attended where you were shoulder to shoulder with everyone.

The story begins with a bleeding woman in desperation. Unable to find healing with resources around her, she pushed up to Jesus and touched the fringe of His garment and immediately received healing. It's important to note that she didn't sit around and sulk in her misery, waiting for someone to reach out to her—which many of us choose to do, hoping that someone out there will see us in our pain and spend time with us. What I also find fascinating is the conversation between Jesus and Peter right after this scene. Luke highlighted it for a reason and we know that every detail in the Bible is intentional.

Jesus first shouted, "Who was it that touched Me?" And Peter, like always, loved to engage Jesus in his unique way. He followed up Jesus' question by saying, "Master, the crowds surround You and are pressing in on You!" In other words, Peter was saying, "Jesus, what are You talking about? There are so many people. Everyone is touching You. Heck, *I'm* touching You." Jesus responded to Peter's comments with, "Someone touched Me, for I perceived that power has gone out from Me" (Luke 8:45–46, author's paraphrase).

Everyone was near Jesus. But only one person came back with a testimony. What made her touch different? She touched Him with *intentionality*.

Jesus obviously knew exactly who touched Him. He knew she was not only struggling with physical illness but emotional and social isolation due to her condition. She couldn't interact with others according to the purity laws, and her pain was much more than physical. She was socially and religiously considered impure. Someone to avoid.

By pausing and highlighting this woman, Jesus was intentionally calling her out of invisibility and connecting with her. She was now seen and known by Jesus Himself (and the crowd). Jesus slowed down and prioritized her. And lastly, Jesus called her "daughter"—a word that signals belonging. The bleeding woman who was rejected, shunned, and isolated from society found belonging again.

As Dr. Curt Thompson said, "We all are born into the world looking for someone looking for us."[6] Throughout the Gospels,

Jesus showed us that most life-giving relationships come through intentionality, not *accidentally*.

- "Come follow me," Jesus said to His disciples (Matthew 4:19 NIV).

  Jesus offered His presence and life to those who weren't even looking for Him.
- "Come down immediately. I must stay at your house today," He told Zacchaeus (Luke 19:5 NIV).

  Jesus was bridging the distance between Zacchaeus and Him.
- To His mother, "Here is your son." To His beloved disciple, "Here is your mother." (John 19:26–27 NIV).

  Jesus was dying on the cross, accomplishing His mission to bring forgiveness, healing, and hope to the entire world. And yet, He was also thinking about His earthly relationships, particularly of His own mother and how she would be cared for after His departure.
- And to all of us: "I have come that [you all] may have life, and have it to the full" (John 10:10 NIV).

  What a beautiful statement that captures the heart of the gospel: God is always chasing and prioritizing us in order that we can have true life. And on the cross, He brought near all who are far away (Ephesians 2:13).

There is so much power in intentionality. In the words of theologian James K. A. Smith, "Discipleship, we might say, is a way to curate your heart, to be attentive to and intentional about what you love."[7] Every morning, we have a fresh opportunity to intentionally say yes to the invitation of Jesus to reprioritize, or to, echoing Augustine and Smith, reorder our loves.

THE ANCIENT WAY

No matter what forces came their way, the early Christians committed themselves to one another as a core value of following Jesus. Luke, the historian, wrote, "They devoted themselves to the apostles' teaching, and the fellowship" (Acts 2:42). The word *devoted* means persistence, consistency, and intentionality. It's a beautiful picture and reminder of the Christian faith in this age of distraction and noncommitment. We give up too quickly and have a low threshold for pain and resilience, but Luke told us the church prioritized and gave their lives around the teachings of Jesus given by the apostles and fellowship.

Let's pause for a second and explore this word *fellowship* or *koinonia* in Greek. The word conveys an active, dynamic participation in relationships, a sharing and giving of ourselves. This is much more than moving in and out of gatherings. *Koinonia* invites us to step out of our comfort zone and self-serving posture and move toward community and communion by serving and meeting the needs of others.

In other words, the early believers resisted the temptation to turn inward instead of outward in their faith. This commitment to and active engagement in the church community wasn't optional. But in our cultural moment, we are facing FOMO (fear of missing out), which makes us believe there is something better "out there." FOMO prioritizes the "next best feeling thing" and reminds us to keep all our options open, whether that be our friends or the local church. This breeds a noncommittal posture and we end up missing out on the very people God has put right in front of us.

SO . . . HOW MANY PEOPLE ARE WE ACTUALLY TALKING ABOUT?

British anthropologist Robin Dunbar argues that humans have a cognitive limit on how many relationships we can maintain: about 150 (known as Dunbar's number). According to the theory, the intimate circle has five people, which is then followed by successive layers of 15 good friends, 50 friends, 150 meaningful contacts, 500 acquaintances, and 1,500 people you can recognize.[8] This will vary slightly by each individual's personality, capacity, and social wiring. My hope and prayer is that this book will help in both identifying and strengthening your core relationships: 1 through 15.

HOW TO PRIORITIZE RELATIONSHIPS

Step 1: Make a List of Significant People in Your Life

I have no idea where you are in your journey of belonging. You may have a ton of people around you or you may have no one. Regardless of where you are, consider taking this first step into experiencing deeper belonging. You can start by identifying key relationships in your life. Even Jesus had a group of twelve who were closest to Him.

At the start of each new year, I spend some time writing in the front of my journal the names of people I would like to prioritize in my life. I pray through who God is highlighting.[9] Again, if you have no one, that's okay. We all start somewhere. You might include a group name (a small group or church community) or region (your neighborhood) instead of an individual. Here is what I've noticed over the years:

1. Some did not reciprocate or make the same prioritization. That's okay (though it's still painful). Move on.

2. Toxic and codependent relationships make it hard to lean into healthy relationships with others. They make you experience a false version of belonging that is actually harmful, abusive, and controlling. Choosing to say no to this group is also a difficult part of this step.

3. Some names have changed, particularly in a new season of life (when we first married, had kids, moved to a new church community, etc.).

4. There were a few surprising names—be open and don't write people off (even those from your past). People do change!

The list doesn't have to be long to belong (see what I did there?). We also need to keep in mind this great reminder from C. S. Lewis about God's intentional placement of people in our lives.

For a Christian, there are, strictly speaking no chances. A secret master of ceremonies has been at work. Christ, who said to the disciples, "Ye have not chosen me, but I have chosen you," can truly say to every group of Christian friends, "Ye have not chosen one another but I have chosen you for one another." The friendship is not a reward for our discriminating and good taste in finding one another out. It is the instrument by which God reveals to each of us the beauties of others.[10]

Wherever God has placed you right now, hold that as sacred ground for belonging. Be careful of the posture of "picking and choosing" as though everyone is at the hands of our mercy. It will condition us to see relationships in a self-serving and transactional way so that we approach connection by asking, "What's in it for me? What can I gain from this person?" Then we will end up limiting our relationships to those who are "useful" to us. However, Lewis reminds us that God's placement is not random but an intentional invitation for us to be watchful and attentive to the particular relationships He has put in our path.

To assess my relationships, I have found it helpful to examine who has historically and consistently "shown up" in times of need. Or I ask myself, *If something were to happen to me right now, who would drop everything and come to my support?*

Once you've identified those you want to be intentional with, you are ready for the next step.

Step 2: Structure Your Time with Others

I'm in a men's group that's been meeting for more than twenty years every Tuesday night at 7:00 p.m. I've been in this group for the last four years. It started when these guys were all single—and like the rest of the world, life happened. They got busy with work. They all got married and had children. And everyone experienced both the highs and the lows of life. Some have moved away and new folks like me joined. But for the most part, the core group of guys has stayed together.

When I joined, I asked them how it had been possible to meet for the last twenty years. They all thought about it and one thing that came up was that they had consistent structure. And now I've been experiencing this power of structure. Let me explain.

Every Tuesday is blocked from 7:00 to 9:30 p.m. on our calendars unless there is a family emergency or vacation/work trip. All our families know that on Tuesday nights we are unavailable. We intentionally have two host homes so that if one host cannot open their home for various reasons, the other host is ready to go. We have a group text thread that asks the same question every Tuesday morning, "Who is in for tonight?" A reminder of our own commitments. This structure kicks in when you are tempted not to show up and move toward self-isolation and comfort.

Priority isn't as simple as prioritizing meaningful belonging—we cannot underestimate the power of structure. We could have the best relationship in the world and the right priorities, but if we do not commit to setting aside a consistent time and space to build on the relationship, it will not develop into something substantial. Intentionality requires structure. In other words, structure will sustain what we value. David Brooks captures it this way: "Thus, the most complete definition of a commitment is this: falling in love with something and then building a structure of behavior around it for those moments when love falters."[11] Or in the words of James Clear, the author of the *New York Times* bestseller *Atomic Habits*: "Goals are good for setting a direction, but systems are best for making progress."[12] If you leave it for "whenever I have time," it will always be "next time." We all have had friends who moved away, and without regular connection we grow apart. We are generally terrible at prioritizing our priorities.

The root word *struct* means to build. When you are building something that will last, it takes time, commitment, and intentionality. When I first joined the staff at my church, I wanted to belong. As I interacted with Andy, Josh, Jay, and Dave, I felt a sense of great connection based on humor, life, ministry, and theology. It was a joy to be with them. However, we were all busy doing ministry and taking care of our families. I longed for deeper and more intentional conversations, but our opportunities were sporadic depending on our availability.

One Thursday, they invited me to join them for lunch at a local Thai restaurant. They shared with me how these Thursday lunches were an intentional time to connect with one another. We had a blast together and I'd desperately needed it. As we were leaving the restaurant, I pulled out my calendar and blocked off every Thursday lunch without an end date. I wanted to be available just in case I got invited again. And thankfully I did and our relationships have taken off since then.

I needed this structure because interruptions happen. Also, agreeing on a repeated connection time saves us the emotional energy of having to ask every week and face potential rejection. I also realized that proximity matters a ton. If this meeting had been forty-five minutes away, it would have been difficult to sustain every week. We normally (before Covid) have the same meeting near the Thai restaurant every Thursday morning so it's easier for us to meet.

Of course, the type of structure varies depending on individual needs. What's easy and simple? Who's right in front of you? What's something everyone would enjoy? Friday afternoon coffee? Tuesday evenings in your home? Sunday morning hike? Wednesday morning after you drop off your kids? Every Monday lunch? (Note: throughout history, eating together has been a safe space for connection and bonding.) Find out what works for you and those you long to prioritize.

If you are already in an intentional small or community group, what would it look like to encourage everyone's commitment and consistency to the group? And if you are new to an area, structure intentionally sows seeds in a community to see which "seeds" will grow. This invisible and hard labor of investing in others by participating, serving, and giving yourself to the needs of others will be tiring in the moment, but will bear the fruit of belonging.

However, we must take care not to reach out in ways that are clingy. Henri Nouwen warns us against that:

> When we feel lonely we keep looking for a person or persons who can take our loneliness away. Our lonely hearts cry out, "Please hold me, touch me, speak to me, pay attention to me." But soon we discover that the person we expect to take our loneliness away cannot give us what we ask for. Often that person feels oppressed by our demands and runs away, leaving us in despair. As long as we approach another person from our loneliness, no mature human relationship can develop. Clinging to one another in loneliness is suffocating and eventually becomes destructive. For love to be possible we need the courage to create space between us and to trust that this space allows us to dance together.[13]

When we try to fill loneliness out of fear, we run into issues like codependency and idolatry. Fear will make us grab and force relationships under the guise of intentionality. A way to avoid this clinginess is to ask ourselves: *Is fear causing me to pursue this relationship to get rid of my loneliness?*

We must do our work by prioritizing belonging and being intentional, but it is God who will give the growth in those relationships. They won't happen fast. There is a reason why God uses agrarian metaphors for growth in the Bible. It takes time. Be patient.

Priority looks like intentionality. Let me share with you our first belonging icon: priority.

Take a moment to visualize who could be in this icon with you. Is there anyone God is inviting you to pay more attention to? Let's review the first practice of belonging: *Priority*.

- People regret not prioritizing their key relationships at the end of their lives.
- The reason we don't prioritize is that other things get in the way (even good things) and our world drives disconnection.
- In the Bible, Jesus prioritized relationships with others by slowing down and making time through intentionality.
- Identify key relationships in your life and create structured time together to foster deeper belonging.

How will you know belonging is blossoming? It's time for the second practice for cultivating belonging: *Chemistry*.

And no, we are not talking about dating.

Priority Reflection

- Think about your friends, community, and key relationships. Who comes to mind that you want to prioritize today?
- What is one regular (weekly) structure you can put in place to help meaningful relationships blossom?

Chapter 4

Practice #2: Chemistry

THE DIFFERENCE BETWEEN *CLIQUE* AND *CLICK*

One of the things I hated most when I was a teenager was feeling left out during youth group meetups in my church. Nobody likes to feel left out, but it was especially painful for me, someone who was still learning American culture. There were cliques and I didn't know how to get into them. I didn't want to look desperate, but I definitely was. After every youth night, I felt that painful longing for someone to say, "Hey, do you want to join us for a game of basketball?" Or "Do you want to grab something to eat?" How great that would have been! But it rarely came. I would wonder, *Are they not listening to these sermons about loving one another, being open, and inviting the stranger? Doesn't the Bible preach against favoritism? Isn't Christian community about breaking down the walls of hostility? And aren't we called to do life with people beyond those who look and think like us?*

This is still the cry of my heart for Christians, and I'm grateful for the clear picture of my calling that came from this early experience. We are missing some of God's very favorite people. And we need to do better for them, and for us.

As a teenager, I vowed that when I became a youth pastor, I would create a biblical culture of belonging and acceptance so those precious kids would not experience what I went through. A few years later, my opportunity arose.

It was a similar group in size to the one I had growing up. Of course, one of the first things I noticed was the established cliques within the group. I felt my calling surge within me and was determined that every student under my care would experience a deep sense of belonging. These cliques would kill my vision of Christian community if I let them stand.

So I did what every great youth pastor would do—I told my student leadership team that one of their primary responsibilities was to be "clique busters." If they saw friends hanging out together, they were to break them apart. It wasn't good to only be with folks you were already comfortable with—those you naturally "click" with. Even during worship services, I forced students to sit with folks they didn't know. Because that's what good Christians did.

It sounded great on paper.

What I ended up doing was breaking apart friendships that were affirming, naturally accepting, and deepening. I couldn't differentiate between cultivating deep relationships that had chemistry and having a closed-off, unwelcoming posture toward others—the subtle yet important distinction between *clique* and *click*. I didn't understand how "natural chemistry" mattered to supernaturally guided Christians.

WAIT—IS THIS EVEN CHRISTIAN?

Let's be honest. Division, hostility, and contempt reign both in and outside the Christian community.

Growing up in Korea, I was taught that all Japanese people were "evil people" for the incredibly harsh treatment we received during their occupation of the Korean peninsula. And I believed it. I would watch soccer games between Korea and Japan, and I would curse Japan out of Korean deep-seated hatred toward them. I'm not naive or dismissive to the trauma and pain of the past. I understand why my ancestors felt that way. But I made a blanket judgment and assumptions against 125 million Japanese people.

These boundary lines have existed throughout history. Jesus received pressure and criticism for eating with sinners and tax collectors and conversing with a Samaritan woman and the poor. Yet He refused to stop connecting with those who were considered "impure" by society and offered belonging to those who didn't think, act, or look like Him.

Paul regularly fought against the spirit of division and an "us versus them" mentality in the first-century Greco-Roman culture. He wrote to the church in Galatia reminding them of the gospel truth: "There is neither Jew nor Greek, there is neither slave nor free, there is no male and female, for you are all one in Christ Jesus" (Galatians 3:28). The things that make us unique and beautiful should not divide us—they should give us the opportunity to celebrate others.

To the church in Corinth, Paul said, "For it has been reported to me by Chloe's people that there is quarreling among you, my brothers. What I mean is that each one of you says, 'I follow Paul,' or 'I follow Apollos,' or 'I follow Cephas,' or 'I follow Christ.' Is Christ divided?" (1 Corinthians 1:11–13).

While I'm for fostering loyalty and security, which creates a deep sense of belonging and community, or a tribe, this type of tribalism lives in stereotypes and judgments of other groups. Steve Bang Lee, one of the lead pastors at Mariners Church, explains that there is a difference between a tribe and tribalism. He said:

- If a tribe is about belonging, tribalism is an unhealthy posture toward those who don't belong.
- If being part of a tribe is about being excited about one's distinctive traits, tribalism is being excited about tearing down what we perceive the other camps have gotten wrong.
- If belonging to a tribe is about forging healthy boundary lines of identity, tribalism is an attitude of war toward those whom we perceive are pursuing a lesser version of Christianity.[1]

Tribalism creates labels and fear and writes people off, creating distance before we have the opportunity to actually know each other. This exists everywhere in our cultural, political, racial, and Christian denominational lines. In our fear and comfort, we create echo chambers by intentionally surrounding ourselves only with those who think, look, and act like us. In the process, we become uncomfortable with those who disagree with us and dismiss God's image-bearers altogether. We dehumanize and even demonize those who do not belong in our echo chamber, and in return, we are losing the art of having conversations and the opportunity to learn, grow, and love well.

Don't fall for this chemistry shortcut: It may seem easier and faster to rally around and build relationships on what we are against rather than on what we are for. Anger, rage, and common enemies are powerful tools that have a way of binding people quickly but they will not last because these are foundations built on sinking sand.

And we may not have to look any further than our own families to recognize hate toward those who believe differently. The Bible makes it clear that the ultimate ethic for His followers is Christian love. According to 1 John, our love is possible because "he first loved us" (4:19). And this love compels us to truly be ministers of reconciliation in our hostile and divided world (2 Corinthians 5). There always seem to be walls of hostility between groups, whether it's over race, gender, socioeconomic, political, or spiritual issues. But Christ commands us to break these man-made walls through the power of love.

Sadly, we are not good at this.

We cannot use chemistry to prevent new possibilities and relationships. The Christian virtue of hospitality isn't a fringe virtue. It was actually quite important to the early church and how they saw and understood what Jesus was doing. The Greek word used in the New Testament for hospitality literally means "love of the stranger." Jesus was criticized by the religious leaders of His day for eating with sinners and tax collectors (Mark 2:15–17). Jesus was open, generous, and service-oriented toward all people.

Author Rosaria Butterfield reminds us: "Our post-Christian neighbors need to hear and see and taste and feel authentic Christianity, hospitality spreading from every Christian home that includes neighbors in prayer, food, friendship, childcare, dog walking, and all the daily matters upon which friendships are built."[2]

We are also called to love our enemies and be with folks who are different from us. Among Jesus' close friends were Simon the Zealot and Matthew the tax collector, who came from opposing extremes in society. Simon wanted to overthrow Rome. Matthew worked for and benefited from Rome. They were enemies but Jesus was making a new community, a community anchored upon His love and His teachings.

"Community," Parker Palmer suggests, "is that place where the person you least want to live with always lives. . . . And when that person moves away, someone else arises immediately to take his or her place."[3] As I write this, I can think of a few in my Christian community who have given me nightmares (and some may say the same about me!). But Jesus teaches, "Love your enemies and pray for those who persecute you" (Matthew 5:44). Jesus takes us beyond loving those who are easy to love to loving those who are at odds with all that we are.

As a pastor focused on discipleship and spiritual formation of the church, I am deeply aware of the danger of the consumeristic, personal-preference-based living that has done so much damage to the followers of Jesus. In his book *Uncomfortable: The Awkward and Essential Challenge of Christian Community*, Brett McCracken correctly argues that the church today is primarily about commitment rather than our comfort (and sadly, extreme commitment gets applied legalistically and even perpetuates abuse).

This is why the order of the five practices is important: We first *prioritize* and commit to others. We do not make sweeping assumptions before getting to know them. And you'd be surprised how some you'd thought you could never have *chemistry* with may become your dearest companions.

Christians are called to love the "unlovable," and no matter how difficult Christian community can be, we must pursue it because He first pursued us. This is what it means to follow Jesus. We are formed into the likeness of the Son as we wrestle together in our differences.

This is the problem: *we confuse the call to love everyone with our journey of belonging.* We usually feel guilty giving more to those we have prioritized because we know our human tendency toward favoritism and comfort. But there is a way to both live a life of love *and* lean into prioritized relationships. Jesus shows us that the two are not at odds.

As we read the Gospels, Jesus was ever so open to the crowd. He taught, served, fed, healed, ministered, and loved the crowd with open arms. Christian community must be open and inclusive to the outsiders as Jesus modeled for us. We should not discriminate based on what the world tells us should divide and separate humans.

At the same time, Jesus clearly chose His close circle of twelve disciples. I wonder how it would've felt to be excluded from the twelve—or from Jesus' inner circle: James, John, and Peter. What if I were part of the twelve but not part of the inner three—how would I feel? They were among the first to be called, witnessed the glorious Transfiguration, and accompanied Jesus in the garden of Gethsemane, in His time of great need. Does this mean Jesus was less loving to others? Was He possibly committing the sin of favoritism?

Should the other disciples have sent a clique-buster team to confront Jesus and the inner three? Of course not.

Jesus was unapologetic in His prioritization and enjoyment of these three disciples. Mark wrote, "And He [Jesus] allowed no one to follow Him except Peter and James and John the brother of James" (5:37). That doesn't sound very "welcoming"! We wonder how Mark felt about this experience.

This is a reminder that human chemistry exists. And it's actually beautiful and needed. Why is there an epidemic of loneliness, and why are so many people having a hard time finding belonging? We have not taught and shared with folks the Bible's beautiful vision of Christian community, a place of true delight in finding, investing in, and doing life with our inner circle. It's not an either/or situation; it's both/and. The vision is to have the crowd, the close twelve, and the closest three *all at the same time.*

Jesus, in the most important moments of His life, leaned into His inner circle. Remember, James, John, and Peter had much in common since they were fishing business partners before being called by Jesus. They shared mutual interests and they probably got along with one another as well. C. S. Lewis said, "People who bore one another should meet seldom; people who interest one another, often."[4] That's chemistry!

Oh, and let's not forget Jesus gave nicknames only to His inner three disciples. Have you ever given out nicknames? When do you generally do that? When there is a deeper bond, right? Jesus called Peter *Cephas*, meaning "Rock," and James and John He called *Boanerges*, which translates to "Sons of Thunder." Have you ever been given a nickname? My nickname in seminary was "mega" because I was loud like a megaphone. (I don't know how to whisper.) And it thrilled me that all my close friends called me by that name. I belonged!

I can't discuss the topic of friendship and chemistry without mentioning one of the most well-known stories in the Bible as an example: David and Jonathan. When our family immigrated to America, David and Jonathan (Jon) became my brother's and my English names. The intentionality behind it stemmed from the fact that we fought a lot growing up. I was six years older and I was mean and selfish. The names were actually given as my poor parents' prayer that we would become great friends! My preschool teacher saw how selfish I was at school and recommended to my parents to have a sibling so I would learn to share. A year later, my brother entered the world due to my sin! I'm so thankful for my brother, Jon, who is my good friend and still teaches me so much about loving others well.

The biblical David and Jonathan appear in 1 Samuel 17, where the young, small David has defeated this great warrior Goliath with God's help, and Saul (the king of Israel and father of Jonathan) has quickly called David to come for a visit. The first verse of chapter 18 says, "As soon as he had finished speaking to Saul, the soul of Jonathan was knit to the soul of David, and Jonathan loved him as his own soul."

Another translation says "there was an immediate bond" between them (TLB). Jonathan got to hear David's heart in the conversation. The Bible says the bond and knitting of the soul happened as soon as David had finished speaking to Saul. I'm certain, knowing David's character, he told Saul about his faith in the living God and said God was the one who gave him the victory. It's reasonable Jonathan's soul knit to David's because they carried similar values, beliefs, and morals.

WHAT IS CHEMISTRY ANYWAY?

We commonly talk about chemistry in romantic relationships. You just "get" each other and there is effortlessness in your conversations. You may share similar interests and values. There seems to be a strong physical or emotional attraction and time tends to go by quickly when you're together. Chemistry is also important in sports in building a team. In soccer, one bad pass can kill the momentum.

Or in basketball, eye contact can communicate to a teammate the next play to make happen. The passer knows exactly when and where to pass, and the scorer knows where the ball will be. There is a natural flow back and forth and connection there—or what we call chemistry.

Interestingly, while it seems like chemistry "just happens," it's actually something we can work to create. Steve Kerr, the Golden State Warriors head coach, who knows about building and leading championship teams, said he uses humor to build chemistry. He creates a fun and playful atmosphere. When we take ourselves less seriously, we let our guards down and we create spaces to connect.

Though humor is a great way to connect, it's not the only way. Shared meals, clear common goals and expectations, and experiencing hardships together all strengthen chemistry. Every good leader knows this: strengthening communication, teamwork, and awareness of self and others increases belonging and team chemistry. It's certainly not an easy process as God has made us with wildly different temperaments, values, personality types, and backgrounds. But with intentional effort, greater chemistry is possible.

In some sense, chemistry is an unexplainable synergy and shared emotional or physical connection between individuals. For those looking for more clarity, don't worry. There is some science to chemistry. First, *brain chemistry*. God designed our brains to release a hormone called oxytocin through social interactions, singing, and physical contact, which enhances feelings of meaningful connection and bond. The more you laugh and sing together, make eye contact, give high-fives and warm hugs, the more you build chemistry.[5]

Second, *friendship chemistry*. The researchers from Cal State University San Bernardino identified the most relevant elements to interpersonal relationships and friendship formation.[6] They found five key factors of friendship chemistry: *reciprocal candor* (really understand each other and can say anything), *mutual interest* (find each other funny and interesting), *personableness* (are warm, caring, and down to earth), *similarity* (share values, beliefs, and morals), and *physical attraction* (it means just that!).

Yet chemistry can often come from only one of these, like having common interests. I wasn't interested in kids' playgrounds and the latest diaper sales until I became a father. My potential chemistry increased with parents who also had young children because we had a mutual interest in kid-related activities and our children's health. It is easier to connect with folks who carry similar values on following Jesus and how we live our lives. Minorities and those who are on the margins of society know how important reciprocal candor is when you meet an ally who gets you and you don't have to explain or justify yourself. And what about personableness? Folks who are kind, respectful, and fun to be around naturally attract others.

Simply, when there is chemistry, you look forward to seeing one another.

CHEMISTRY AS DISCOVERY

With the church I serve, we have the wonderful step in our discipleship process of sharing our life stories. In smaller groups with a pastor/coach, people share their highs and lows, key moments, how they came to Jesus, and where they are now in faith. I can't tell you enough how many divine connections and sparked conversations have been made naturally by sharing a bit of who we are.

In a recent story time I led with four ladies, one shared about her journey of following Jesus in stage 4 cancer. Then another woman shared that she was battling against stage 4 as well. We wept together. We also learned that one of them had been unsuccessful in a past suicide attempt, and that two others had been suicidal as well, but by God's grace, they had survived. None of us knew each other before that gathering, but by the time it was over, we'd never forget each other.

It's a gift to continually recognize how similar our stories are. C. S. Lewis, in *The Four Loves*, puts it this way:

> Friendship arises out of mere companionship when two or more of the companions discover that they have in common some insight or interest or even taste which the others do not share and which, till that moment, each believed to be his own unique treasure (or burden). The typical expression of opening friendship would be something like, "What? You too? I thought I was the only one."[7]

I love that. I think our group said "What? You too?" over and over again in that meeting.

Of course, some groups don't share as much in common, and some even have stark differences. But it's important not to feel guilty or take it personally if there is disagreement. In Acts, Luke observed that the great early church leaders Paul and Barnabas had a sharp disagreement, then went separate ways:

> Some time later Paul said to Barnabas, "Let us go back and visit the believers in all the towns where we preached the word of the Lord and see how they are doing." Barnabas wanted

to take John, also called Mark, with them, but Paul did not think it wise to take him, because he had deserted them in Pamphylia and had not continued with them in the work. They had such a sharp disagreement that they parted company. Barnabas took Mark and sailed for Cyprus, but Paul chose Silas and left. (Acts 15:36–40 NIV)

Both Paul and Barnabas loved Jesus but had a different perspective on John Mark. Paul was being cautious of John Mark's past actions, while Barnabas wanted to give him another chance. We can love one another *and* go separate ways. It's okay to have our own preferences and not take everything personally.

I find it helpful that when we hire staff at our church, we remind them our relationship is now both covenantal and contractual. If there comes a time to terminate the contractual aspect of a relationship for whatever reason, we are still committed to the covenantal relationship—our ongoing commitment to pray for, care for, and love one another in the name of Jesus. We should not confuse the two.

I think of the discovery phase as a jigsaw puzzle. My wife and my two girls love puzzles, but I'm terrible at them. My impatience makes me give up quickly. Sometimes I try to help and put in pieces that don't belong, and it's awkward. I know each piece has its place, but it may not be the one you need now. That's *okay*. All stories and all people belong, but the journey is to find where you belong most.

Only when it's not forced will it find its perfect place in the larger puzzle. And when it does, it's a beauty to behold. Some of us need to be freed from the guilt and shame that we aren't doing enough equally for everyone. Allow yourself the permission, process, and joy of finding your people. Here is another look at the second belonging icon: chemistry.

TAKE CARE WHEN MIXING (OR NAVIGATING) DIFFICULT PEOPLE, INCLUDING YOU

If you've taken a chemistry class, you know how important correct mixtures are. My friend Dave's chemistry teacher passed out in high school because he mixed the wrong chemical during a class demonstration! The students had to open all the windows to remove the toxic gas.

Such dangers don't just happen in chemistry classrooms. Some chemistry explosions happen in relationships, and they harm everyone near them, causing damage that requires much healing.

There are several toxic traits to watch out for. People who exhibit them require unusually good boundaries and relational skills—or they may need to be avoided altogether. And, yes, we can forgive others as followers of Jesus and still hold healthy boundaries.

- *People who overtalk*
  They constantly babble to fill the conversation with their words. They don't know how to listen and they drain the energy of everyone around them.

- *People who bring everything back to themselves*
  They are generally self-absorbed and might also use others for their own benefit. They can be tough to spot because they use their charisma to draw attention or gain power, and they can become abusive and controlling.
- *People who criticize often*
  To be around them is to feel judged or criticized. They are generally uptight and often turn everything into a teaching lesson. They may love drama or take themselves very seriously. They are not fun to be around.
- *People who victimize themselves*
  They usually don't mean to make it all about them. They simply believe they carry so much burden that they need to unload onto others all the time. Victims believe the world is against them and their defense is to be constantly "moody." Are you always walking on thin ice around them? Well, then, you know a victim.

There is nothing that kills chemistry like interacting with people with the traits above. The common factor in all four types is that they make it all about *them.* You could have amazing chemistry with a group, but if someone with any of those strong traits joins, it could potentially kill the momentum. Of course, without God's help, we're all susceptible to those traits. If people frequently withdraw from you, then you might want to take an honest self-assessment and consider what is driving you—or consider seeking help from a therapist.

Think back to the potential names or groups you identified in the last chapter on priority. Below are some practical steps to see if there might be some chemistry to form bonds.

CHEMISTRY EXPERIMENTS: FOUR STEPS

1. Stay curious about other people's stories.

We regularly rush toward judgment and assumptions, writing people off and limiting our opportunity for connection. There is nothing that draws people faster than someone who takes an interest in them. There is nothing more disarming and inviting than saying to someone, "Tell me more about your story!"

2. Identify your values.

Whether in your workplace, marriage, friendships, or Christian community, it's important to find people with whom you share core values that help create chemistry. Without shared values, most relationships will ultimately break down, and it will be difficult to form deep belonging. More than that, toxic belonging can undo us: "Do not be deceived: 'Bad company ruins good morals'" (1 Corinthians 15:33). We become like those we spend time with. So take some time to evaluate your top core values and the kind of person you'd like to be. (Note: Our values do change. This is why we shouldn't feel guilty about not being able to maintain friends from our past.)

3. Check yourself after being with others.

Ask yourself questions: Is my tank full after spending time with them? Was it life-giving? Do I miss them? Do I feel encouraged after being with them?

4. Try new things.

A few years into our marriage, my wife and I found ourselves at odds in terms of our mutual interests. The more we got to know each other, the more we realized that we liked the exact opposite things. And that was totally okay—except that we didn't have common grounds for connection and bonding. She listened to weird indie sleepy music. I loved K-pop music. She loved good loose-leaf tea and boba. I loved single-origin drip coffee. She loved watching *The Office*—she's probably on her tenth time through the entire series by now! I loved zombies and action movies. So we tried new things together and discovered that we enjoyed playing board games and doing escape rooms.

Connect with others based on interests, such as finding a local cafe where you can discuss a book together. Remember, we can work to develop chemistry, like teams and organizations foster chemistry within their groups.

Ready for our next practice? This one comes with potentially even greater dangers. But I think you'll find it's worth the risk.

Chemistry Reflection

- Name your top two core values.
- Who do you generally enjoy spending time with? Why?
- Identify your top three pet peeves in relationships. Refer back to the section "Take Care When Mixing" to see if any of those are included.
- Is there a group of people you have distanced yourself from or have not given much of a chance? What if the very community you are looking for is in that group? What would it look like to let your guard down and open yourself up to a conversation?

Chapter 5

Practice #3: Vulnerability

LOWERING THE WALL OF SHAME

FOR CONNECTION

W hen I was living on Long Island, I remember asking my mom to drop me off three blocks away from my high school.

"Why so far away, David?" she asked, genuinely puzzled.

"I want to get in some exercise before school starts."

I'm pretty certain she knew I was lying, but I didn't have the courage to tell her the real reason.

You see, our family of four survived on a pastor's tiny salary in New York City. Each paycheck barely paid our monthly bills. And the only vehicle we had was a beat-up 1997 Toyota Corolla. For me, our car was a reminder of my family's relative poverty compared to the other kids. I was embarrassed. I didn't want people to know that I was so poor. I wanted to be accepted—and pulling up in a crummy, Christmas-green, beat-up clunker was *not* going to help that cause.

This wasn't some imagined slight from a hypersensitive immature kid. I had data. I regularly saw how poor kids were treated in the school. Other kids made fun of their off-brand clothes or their weathered shoes or their tattered winter jackets. If this was social Darwinism, the poor kids were the gazelles getting torn into by the pride of lionesses. I had to hide that part of my life's story. It was a matter of survival. *I longed to be seen and known.* But I had no idea how to make that happen. So I hid. Even walking ten minutes out of my way every single day.

What I've come to learn is that humans are really, really good at hiding. We've been practicing since the beginning.

In the very first pages of the Bible, Adam and Eve were both naked, and they felt no shame (Genesis 2:25). But as soon as sin entered the story, they covered themselves and hid from God. Yet, He didn't respond with, "What the heck did you two do? I only left for a second!" Instead He asked where they were, a gentle, invitational question for conversation and connection, meant more for them than Himself.

But it didn't matter. Shame had kicked in. Adam responded, "I was afraid, because I was naked, and I hid myself" (Genesis 3:10). Now, before we blame Adam and Eve for ruining things, remember, we all do this. We put up walls for self-protection. We put the blame on others, and we refuse to take responsibility. Shame, fear of being disconnected and alone, is the very thing that prevents us from pursuing deep relationships.[1] We are desperate for connection, yet feel profound shame for needing it. So we hide from God and each other hoping to avoid more shame and rejection. And in the process, we get really good at hiding many parts of ourselves.

Perhaps you can relate. When guests come over to your house, do you try to make it as clean as possible? In my house, we work our way from the living room to the kitchen, then our bathroom, and lastly our girls' room. As we clean what we don't want others to see, we sometimes hide the big stuff in our bedroom. Our friends won't be going in there, so we simply close that door. It's convenient. No one needs to know.

And we do this with our lives—hiding our messes—and we get used to this lifestyle.

But let me ask you: Have you ever hidden something so well that you can't find it?

I have. Many times. And it's incredibly frustrating, especially when I need that important shirt, or gift, or document—immediately. When we hide parts of ourselves regularly enough, we shouldn't be surprised when it becomes harder to find them.

THE QUESTION WE ALL SECRETLY ASK OURSELVES

When I lived in Boston for college, sometimes people would yell things out to me from their car window.

"Go back to your country!"

This kind of thing used to happen to me a lot when I was younger. It was always a painful reminder to me that my "Asianness" was preventing me from belonging.

But honestly, it's not those overt examples of drive-by racism that have been the most painful. It's been the tiny comments. Sometimes these are called micro-aggressions—small comments that seem well-meaning but that actually imply something is wrong with the other person. Comments like "Where are you really from?"—which highlighted that I wasn't from New York. Or, "Are you from North or South Korea?" I'd think to myself, *Um, you realize that nobody gets out of North Korea because it's a totalitarian state whose borders are on military lockdown, right?* When I was a kid in elementary school, the other kids would comment in the cafeteria about my lunch.

"Wow, your food is stinky!" they'd say, smelling the different spices that are so integral to Korean dishes.

I tried to hide my Korean-ness. I stopped bringing Korean food to lunch. I tried to conceal my Korean accent. I tried to hide my love for K-Pop. I even felt my Korean heritage slowly become a source of shame for me, and I worked to distance myself from it. At some point, I started to forget Korean words and the beauty of Korean Christian spirituality that significantly shaped my faith. I didn't know at the time, but I was assimilating to be accepted into the majority culture.

In some ways, hiding is what we all do. We hide what is lacking and change what is different in order to belong. We end up walking around with a false version of ourselves—the false self. Then the question becomes, who am I really? Spiritual director and author Alice Fryling wrote,

The false self is the person we think we should be but are not. It is the person we want others to think we are. The false self perpetuates the illusion that we are able to love perfectly, to be wise and all-knowing, and to be in control of life. The false self thrives on success and achievement. The problem is not that the false self is a bad person. The problem is that the false self is a façade. It is an imitation of God that we "use" to impress others. The false self languishes in pretense and in grasping for abilities and gifts that are not ours to have.[2]

We quickly figure out what is accepted in our workplace, our church, our friendships, and family and we hide everything else. We have to in order to belong, and we believe we are not enough, or too much. We don't fit. This can lead to imposter syndrome—feelings of inadequacy crippled by fear of exposure—and we are afraid of people finding out that we aren't somehow truly "qualified" to belong in this particular environment. So we become perfectionistic, insecure, and anxious trying to manage the charade. And for many, there are some things we never tell *anyone*. In fact, sometimes we isolate even further to prevent others from finding out.

But here is the real question we all secretly ask ourselves: "Where does *all* of me belong? My true self?" We wonder if we'll ever be loved for who we are, what we believe, and what we have or haven't done. The pain of being alone, unseen, overlooked, and dismissed is too great to stay where we are. So we make efforts to come out of hiding. We long for a deeper connection with others. This is how God wired us. The final verse of Genesis 2 before the fall captures humanity's design for connection and relationship in this way: "Adam and his wife were both naked, and they felt no shame" (Genesis 2:25 NIV).

Hebrew Bible scholar Carissa Quinn explains, "In other words, the ideal picture is one of relational safety, vulnerability, trust and acceptance of the other."[3] We long for what has been taken away by the fall.

This process of coming out of hiding is called *vulnerability*. Through such authenticity, we find answers to that deepest question. Vulnerability means allowing your authentic self to be seen, including your honest thoughts and emotions. It could be about sharing your struggles in marriage. It might be saying no when something doesn't fit you. Asking someone out on a date in confidence, regardless of their response. Confessing a sin that you'd rather hide from. Talking about your failures and mistakes as you go through them. Sharing about your own needs. We lower the walls around our hearts and invite others in, in hopes of love and embrace. When it happens, we experience greater belonging.

DO YOU WANT TO GRAB LUNCH?

I want to admit something to you. Even with my close friends, I get nervous right before I text to ask if they would like to grab lunch with me. I don't want to look desperate. And I definitely don't want to experience all the different ways they might say no. My anxiety heightens every time I check my phone after I send that text. Silence makes it worse. I then begin to write a different script in my head for each person so I can feel better about myself: *They haven't had time to check their phone yet. He probably has an important lunch meeting.* But sometimes in my negative scripts, I think, *Maybe I shouldn't have asked. I bet they have a better offer from someone cooler.* Vulnerability doesn't feel comfortable. It sometimes feels like losing control.

Drs. John and Julie Gottman, world-renowned psychologists and relationship experts, would call my texts for lunch "Bids for Connection."[4] Bids are gestures that signal our need for attention and connection. We long for every bid to turn toward (acknowledge/accept) us but when someone turns away (misses) or turns against (rejects) our vulnerable bid for connection, it can be devastating.

Vulnerability certainly doesn't guarantee amazing outcomes. This is why it's so difficult to be vulnerable. We all have had experiences where we were hurt and ignored by family, friends, coworkers, and Christian community. We've been misunderstood, judged wrongly, and taken advantage of. These feelings of shame, rejection, and unpredictability ultimately prevent us from fully living our lives. So we stop "bidding" altogether because we are tired of getting disappointed again.

C. S. Lewis famously put it this way:

There is no safe investment. To love at all is to be vulnerable. Love anything, and your heart will certainly be wrung and possibly be broken. If you want to make sure of keeping it intact, you must give your heart to no one, not even to an animal. Wrap it carefully round with hobbies and little luxuries; avoid all entanglements; lock it up safe in the casket or coffin of your selfishness. But in that casket—safe, dark, motionless, airless—it will change. It will not be broken; it will become unbreakable, impenetrable, irredeemable.[5]

He nods to this risk-taking that comes with vulnerability and reminds us that there is indeed another way to live. We can choose to live a life in such a way as to never get hurt. But to Lewis's point, are we then really living?

CULTURAL CHALLENGES
TO VULNERABILITY

We all live within an existing culture of some sort, which comes with obstacles to vulnerability. This isn't an exhaustive list, but here are some key forces to consider.

Personal Pain and Trauma

We all have our own stories of pain. Those might come from experiences with abuse—including violence, neglect, silencing, gossip, backstabbing, emotional, physical, and spiritual manipulation—or, in my case, with racism and relative poverty that affects mental health and well-being. Sadly, it's still taboo and a source of shame in many contexts to talk about our story.

Personality

We use our personality types to excuse ourselves from being vulnerable. "I'm more of an independent, logic-and-facts-based person. I prefer to keep things to myself. That's just the way I am." We keep our guards up and keep people at arm's length.

Family of Origin

What was modeled at home for us? Did our parents share their mistakes, show their weaknesses, and process their fears, hopes, and dreams? If the home isn't a safe place to be comforted, shown grace and mercy, and observe a model of emotional vulnerability, for our own safety we often learn not to share how we are really doing.

Digital Media

In our digital age, we have more opportunities to hide our identities as we send our feedback and critiques to others. We can hide behind our screens and stay anonymous in those human connections. We get so used to using "filter" and "polish" options on social media that we end up using them outside of our digital devices.

Pace of Life

In a busy, efficiency-based society, we tend to avoid anything that will slow our progress. We complain about how long a six-hour flight is from New York to San Francisco when for most of human history, it took months to make that journey! Any meaningful processing of our motives and desires would require space and time. We believe that *results* are what matter, much more than the *process*. It's easier to constantly distract ourselves by performing than to do the slow work of excavating what we have buried inside.

It is also messier to choose vulnerability. When we open up and share honestly about how we truly feel, it opens doors for uncomfortable conversations. We cannot determine how others will respond. It's risky. We could be misunderstood and even rejected. Some of us hate burdening others with what we are going through. Sometimes we don't even know what's going to come out of our mouths when we let our guards down. Many of us hate surprises, especially from ourselves. Who wants to lose control, be a burden, or be seen as emotional or sensitive? So instead, we cover ourselves.

Eastern vs. Western Culture

As a bicultural kid, a Korean American, I have experienced the cultural forces of both the East and West. The East is primarily a shame and honor culture. "Saving face"—meaning giving someone an opportunity to avoid embarrassment, humiliation, or shame—is a central value. Public dignity and image matter a lot. Malcolm Gladwell in his book *Outliers* examines how Korean Air had more plane crashes than almost any other airline at the end of the 1990s. He correctly points out that the reason was not due to lack of training or skill but to the hierarchical, shame and honor culture that makes it incredibly difficult to speak up to a supervisor, even if it costs their lives![6]

Even with our education and career choices, we were often limited by our family's desires. The question we all asked was "What will bring our family the most honor?" It generally revolves around the big three: doctor, lawyer, or engineer. We were taught that saying what we really want is selfish. It's always about seeking what's best for the family, the group, the organization. Vulnerability is further complicated in Eastern culture in that one's identity is connected to and found in the community, whereas, in the West, it's solely on the individual. For example, in the West, your last name is your family name. In the East, your family name is your first name. This captures the reality that individual identity is a special challenge for those in the Eastern culture. And even as I write this, I'm constantly considering what stories to share in this book and whether some of my stories may bring shame to my parents and our larger family.

For Westerners, vulnerability is often seen as weakness. Americans are taught to look and be strong. Sayings like "don't be so sensitive" or "suck it up" prevent honesty and don't allow us to process our emotions. We want to look self-sufficient and not needy in any way. We don't want others to think we are a mess, and even if we haven't figured it all out, we still know to only share once it's presentable. Many people have a very hard time even asking for help. We don't want to look incompetent. So we hide our weaknesses. In addition, our hyper-individualized society places a high value on personal privacy and has a "we keep things to ourselves" attitude that makes it hard to go beyond the surface.

Certainly, globalization has made these East/West values more nuanced depending on where you live. It gets even more complex with *gender* (stereotypes that real men or ideal women aren't emotional), *age* (you should have figured this out by now), and *title* (how do you not know that in your position?) expectations. When we don't live up to the expectations of society or of those around us, when we don't fit a certain mold, we hide in shame or force ourselves to fit the mold.

But there is even more.

CHRISTIAN CHALLENGES TO VULNERABILITY

Sadly, there is an added layer of challenges that come to Christians in our journey of vulnerability and belonging.

We-Don't-Talk-About-This Topics

In your Christian community (or at home), are there topics that are off-limits to talk about? When Christian community shames or condemns even discussing certain things, it's a painful reminder that certain sins or sinners are too sinful to be spoken of aloud. Therefore, it's too risky to bring it up.

I received a call from my buddy Jon who is married with kids. He shared with me his frustrations about his relationship with money and admitted that he had never properly filed taxes because money was seen as too evil to talk about in his home.

In my Eastern tradition, I've noticed some topics are consistently taboo, including

- Personal finances
- Sexuality and sexual history
- Mental health
- Race and politics
- Addictions
- Doubts about faith
- Senior leadership accountability

Which topics have you been told *not* to talk about?

Dismissive Spiritual Talk

There are certain statements we can use to quickly dismiss and minimize how we really think and feel. We override ourselves and others in the name of God, the Bible, and the cross. It's tricky because they usually sound spiritual. But they are half-truths and quite dismissive in the journey of vulnerability.

WE USE GOD:
Definitely seeking God on that one! (I've already told Jesus about it, so I'm good to go.)

Hey, God's got this! Don't want to be guilty of not
    trusting God!
Don't want to worry about anything and risk missing His
    blessing!

WE USE THE BIBLE:

I want to focus only on the truth.
It is not about what I feel but what the Bible says.

WE USE THE CROSS:

Jesus already paid it all. No need to look to the past!
There is more victory, joy, and your best life up ahead!

Again, such statements may be true, but they can make it extra difficult to engage in conversations that are honest, real, and sincere. This generally plays out in two ways. First, the *Jesus juke*. It ends up killing the conversation because we are not curious about the other person. We care about our agenda only. Second, *minimization of sin*. We believe sin isn't a big deal so it's not worth bringing up—but Jesus certainly saw it as a big deal.

The Holiness Game

Christian community can silently play what I call the Holiness Game, where we try to show others how godly we are. I have friends I've known for a long time who rarely share their struggles and only talk about the wins in their lives with God. Any vulnerability jeopardizes our image and reputation as "mature followers" of Jesus, so it is too risky. Worse, the game can become advanced by using *fake* vulnerability to appear more #authentic. Fake vulnerability includes manipulation, carefully picking and choosing the appearance of sharing the real while the heart behind it is more for attention and applause for looking more godly than for being real.

There's even *Holiness Game 2.0*, a more aggressive version where you straight-up use holiness to rebuke and cancel people. Completely disregarding kindness, grace, love, and nearly all other key virtues of the Christian faith, people create real fear in those near them, hindering any confession and vulnerability.

I know the *Holiness Game 2.0* because I played it in my early years of youth ministry. I would get so angry and upset with people's sins—but I insisted it was godly, holy anger. In reality, I was covering up my own sins by focusing on the sins of other people.

Lack of Authentic Vulnerability Modeled by Leaders

The Latin root word for *vulnerability* is "capable of being wounded." It's intimidating when we see a "perfect" family, marriage, and faith through the filtered pages of social media or in the pulpit. If we see people who have their lives together, we might fall into the trap of comparison and think, *What am I doing wrong? How can I be more like them? How do they never fight? How are all their examples success stories?*

I asked one pastor why he doesn't share anything personal in his sermons—about his family, marriage, struggles, personal fears, and hopes. He said the sermon should only be about the Bible and Jesus, not about him. There is some wisdom in this, yet I wonder if, in this "godly" answer and his theological framework, he is actually afraid he will lose credibility if he shares about his failures or will not be respected enough.

No one is a 24/7 success story! Consider the effects when

people are silenced and the truth is covered up so frequently after misconduct or abuse by the same leaders who were supposed to protect and care for those they were leading. How can anyone in that environment truly be vulnerable? They say it's all for the sake of "honoring your leaders" and "kingdom work" and any challenges to their character are met with the famous three Ds: denial, defensiveness, and dishonesty.

Not only are they not vulnerable, some leaders use vulnerability for emotional manipulation and their gain (financial giving, greater applause, and more). Of course, not every smiling person is a crook. There are so many sincerely good people in ministry. Still, it can be extremely hard to spot a fake.

Add in gossip, backstabbing, condemnation, and criticisms from both in and out of the church, and it's a lot. All of this breaks trust and opens us up to more pain. Who really wants to sign up for vulnerability with all that?

But there is hope!

THE ADVANTAGE

Christians have a unique advantage when it comes to vulnerability.

We know that God doesn't reject us. We may still retreat and hide like Adam and Eve, afraid of what God might say and do to us when we fall short. Yet the Bible says that we are made in the image of God and are fully loved by Him as His children. It's true there is nothing in our lives, no matter how shameful, that Jesus' finished work on the cross cannot forgive and restore. We can find refuge and strength through Him. Author and pastor Rich Villodas reminds us:

Adam and Eve hid behind a tree, naked and conquered by
shame.
But Jesus hung on a tree, naked, and conquered shame.
In Jesus, shame doesn't have the last word.[7]

Jesus offers healing to what has been lost from the fall: relational connection.

Belonging is so conditional in our society that our belonging to God is also conditioned by this perspective. Romans 5:8, one of my favorite verses, says, "But God demonstrates his own love for us in this: While we were still sinners, Christ died for us" (NIV). God sees and knows all of us, including our hidden parts. And yet He loves us fully and unconditionally. Our identity and hope come from being anchored in this gospel truth. We belong to God and nothing can separate us from His everlasting love. Therefore, we can confidently approach God's throne of *grace*, not condemnation, rejection, or shame.

This is why as an Asian American, male, Christian pastor, I can either choose to be crippled by the forces of shame, pride, and expectations that each category offers, or drink from the fountain of God's love and acceptance that allows me to be honest in my struggle with people-pleasing tendencies and human approval.

Jesus Models Vulnerability

We can be comforted knowing Jesus also experienced much shame and rejection here on earth. John wrote, "He [Jesus] was in the world, and though the world was made through him, the world did not recognize him. He came to that which was his own, but his own did not receive him" (John 1:11 NIV). Jesus opened Himself to others but was frequently met with rejection and hostility. Indeed, God's becoming human, making Himself available, relinquishing power and control, and initiating this intimate relationship are His great acts of vulnerability. It's hard for some of us to be vulnerable because that requires surrendering our control, which can lead to hurt and disappointment. Jesus invites us again and again to trust Him and not let our fears control and rob us of life to the fullest.

Jesus became vulnerable for our good.

There is a fascinating scene in the Gospel of John when Martha and Mary told Jesus that their brother Lazarus had died. Notice the emotions of Jesus:

> When Jesus saw her weeping, and the Jews who had come along with her also weeping, he was deeply moved in spirit and troubled. "Where have you laid him?" he asked. "Come and see, Lord," they replied. Jesus wept. Then the Jews said, "See how he loved him!" But some of them said, "Could not he who opened the eyes of the blind man have kept this man from dying?"
> (John 11:33–37 NIV)

If Jesus allowed His spirit and emotions to be stirred, even weeping and being vulnerable to feel the loss of His friend and the sorrow of death, surely we are encouraged to grieve our losses and join with others in their pain. From His deep love for His friend, Jesus was troubled.

Jesus could have skipped all this emotional vulnerability. One may think, *Why not just get right to it, Jesus? You have the power to resurrect Lazarus from the dead. Why take the time to feel grief?* Logically, emotions make no sense. Many of us criticize even our own emotions. We believe we should be concerned with facts and "the truth." But our feelings matter, too, and Jesus modeled this illogical vulnerability.

John records how differently two groups responded to Jesus' vulnerability. The Jews said, "See how he loved him!" (v. 36). For them, Jesus' vulnerability showed His love and care. But some said, "Could not he who opened the eyes of the blind man have kept this man from dying?" (v. 37). This emotionless question attempted to blame Jesus for not coming to heal Lazarus. Even for Jesus, vulnerability had two different results!

The Bible Demands We Do the Same

The Bible is filled with stories that model a life of vulnerability. Even Jesus, right before His death, prayed an honest prayer that makes some Christians slightly uncomfortable. "Father, if you are willing, remove this cup from me. Nevertheless, not my will, but yours, be done" (Luke 22:42). Still, we try to justify His prayer theologically instead of allowing Jesus to be human.

The apostle Paul said, "I do not understand what I do. For what I want to do I do not do, but what I hate I do" (Romans 7:15 NIV). What a statement. And what an encouragement to all of us. If the apostle Paul, who wrote thirteen of the twenty-seven books of the New Testament, could say this about his own faith journey, we can be honest about our struggles and weaknesses.

As representatives of God in this world (2 Corinthians 5:18–20), we are called to accept one another just as Christ accepted us (Romans 15:7). We are instructed to confess to one another and pray for each other that we may be healed (James 5:16). And though incredibly difficult, we are called to ask for and offer forgiveness because Jesus offers us grace in every moment of our lives. There is beautiful healing in the context of community. The act of repentance is vulnerable. We are acknowledging that we don't have it together and that we need help. And we are invited to do this regularly with God and others (Luke 17:4). In doing so, we are recognizing how serious and destructive sin is and how powerful the gospel is.

In my belonging journey, I have been grateful for Eugene and Dan. In my first small group, they consistently modeled what true vulnerability looks like. I came in with all the what-ifs: *What if they judge me because I'm a pastor? What if my sins are leaked out? What if they reject me from the community?* My hesitation and doubts were met with their transparency and safety over and over again. And soon, simply being in the same room with similar struggles, I was encouraged to both name and explore my root issues with compassion. Brené Brown captures what I was feeling at that time (and still do): "Vulnerability is the last thing I want you to see in me, but the first thing I look for in you."[8]

I began to make sense of what the apostle Paul meant when he said, "Because we loved you so much, we were delighted to share with you not only the gospel of God but our lives as well" (1 Thessalonians 2:8 NIV). Eugene and Dan taught me as pastors and church leaders—in our love and commitment to one another—we can share both the gospel and our lives with one another.

Over the years, I have had the honor of leading or participating in premarital or marital counseling, small groups, addiction and support groups, and retreats and conferences where, sometimes for the first time, people are sharing something they've kept inside their entire lives. And in the midst of their pain, tears, fears, shaky voices and hands, I can also see them experiencing *life*. True freedom, joy, and healing in Christ. Jesus reminds us we all need Him. In the words of Dietrich Bonhoeffer, "Only the

Christian knows this. In the presence of a psychiatrist I can only be a sick man; in the presence of a Christian brother I can dare to be a sinner."[9]

Vulnerability isn't only confession of sins but also learning to own and tell our stories truthfully. (*Alethia—truth* in Greek— literally means "unhiddenness.") It's being honest with where we are and where we'd like to be. This happens in all sorts of ways, including during baptisms. Why is it that we feel so close as a church and to those sharing their testimony during this time? Because of *vulnerability*. So much of the testimony revolves around "this is who I once was, my life revolved around these things, but now I say yes to Jesus and will follow after Him." In vulnerability, we come to learn we are all sinners, saved by the grace of Jesus, and now have the same mission and purpose in life: to live a life surrendered to Jesus. It's saying I don't have everything together but I am declaring that, with His help, I will follow Jesus.

Take your time. God is patient with us. Remember, forced vulnerability is abuse. Only when you are ready and the Spirit of God is leading you, go for it.

Vulnerability isn't safe but it creates safety. I call it "dangerously safe" because vulnerability truly sets hearts free and offers belonging.

Here is the third belonging icon: vulnerability.

For the ancient Israelites, *lev*, which is translated from Hebrew as "heart," meant your thoughts, emotions, affections, feelings, desires, and wills. It is the *center*, the innermost being of who you are.

As we come out of hiding through vulnerability, by fully opening ourselves—our *lev*—in wisdom, we experience freedom, healing, and opportunity to be seen, known, and loved in even deeper ways. And vulnerability offers this incredible emotional intensity that binds together those who are near it. Hence, we increase in *belonging*.

Paul's invitation rings as true to all the followers of Jesus now as it was to the church of Corinth. "We have spoken freely to you, Corinthians, and *opened wide our hearts* to you. We are not withholding our affection from you, but you are *withholding yours* from us. As a fair exchange—I speak as to my children—*open wide your hearts* also" (2 Corinthians 6:11–13 NIV, emphasis added).

GROWING YOUR VULNERABILITY MUSCLES: EIGHT EXERCISES

1. Develop a right view of God.

A. W. Tozer reminds us that "what comes into our minds when we think about God is the most important thing about us."[10] When our view of God is twisted—*He will never forgive me* or *I'm certain He is an angry, cranky, and abusive Being*—it's hard to come to Him honestly. One parable that Jesus Himself shared to shape our view of God is Luke 15:11–32, known as the parable of the lost son. I encourage you to pause here, look it up, and take some time to slowly read and reflect on this story.

2. Name your fears.

It's more than knowing truths about God's grace. We have to name and work through our shame to confidently receive His grace. In my years of pastoral ministry, I've noticed that people, including myself, generally have a harder time experiencing the latter. Curt Thompson wrote, "The question is not do you know this as a fact but rather do you feel it in your bones? . . . [If not], it has not taken up residency as robustly as God intends."[11]

What are some of your specific challenges that prevent vulnerability? Ask Jesus to both reveal them and strengthen you. What's one thing you'd rather not talk about—and why? Pray with the psalmist, "Search me, God, and know my heart" (Psalm 139:23 NIV). In other words, what are you ashamed of? Shame has a way of crippling our identity and worth, and our ability to be honest. Once you've named it, you can begin the journey of learning what the root causes might be, the deep wounds of your heart—then invite Jesus for guidance and healing.

And when you are able, face that very difficult question: *What sin am I intentionally hiding?*

Covering up sin is detrimental to our souls and to our relationships with God and others. My pastor Steve said, "A lot of people think that getting away with sin is God's grace . . . but it's not. That's what the Enemy wants. The grace of God is not getting away with sin; the grace of God is confession."[12]

3. Stop hiding.

If you are frustrated that there isn't much to share and you believe you aren't hiding anything, that might signal a lack of self-understanding. And that's okay! We all start somewhere. There are many great tools to help increase self-awareness and to excavate stored-up pain and stories. Find someone who is further down the road in terms of navigating the unknown terrains of the soul to help you get started.

4. Embrace your weakness and limits.

Paul tried to get rid of his thorn but God reminded him, "My grace is sufficient for you, for my power is made perfect in weakness." Paul responded, "Therefore I will boast all the more gladly about my weaknesses, so that Christ's power may rest on me. That is why, for Christ's sake, I delight in weaknesses, in insults, in hardships, in persecutions, in difficulties. For when I am weak, then I am strong" (2 Corinthians 12:9–10 NIV). Our weaknesses and limitations are reminders of our humanity and the gift of grace for us to depend on God.

The great novelist and spiritual writer Flannery O'Connor said, "[To] know oneself is, above all, to know what one lacks. It is to measure oneself against Truth and not the other way around. The first product of self-knowledge is humility."[13] We often try to hide or overcompensate for our shortcomings and weaknesses. When we can humbly accept our own limits, we become less self-critical and defensive, and more willing to accept help from others.

5. Fight well.

In our journey of belonging, we will quickly realize conflict is inevitable. The point is not to avoid conflict, but to go through conflict well. When it's done poorly, relationships are damaged and in some cases broken. It's easier for us to naturally respond with one of the Four Dysfunctions of belonging (from chapter 2)— being avoidant, anxious, aggressive, or accommodating—because they don't require vulnerability. These dysfunctions become our own damaging fight patterns and, if left unchecked, can break the relationships we treasure. Think back to how many relationships you may have lost due to unresolved or poorly managed conflict.

Conflict is always difficult, but when it's done well it can lead to even deeper bonds and connections. We can come out with a greater understanding, care, and appreciation for each other—thereby creating even more trust. So how do you "fight well"? Healthy conflict always requires vulnerability—courage to be honest and face *all* of it. It's saying, "Hey, you are important to me and I would like for us to work through this together."

How do you normally deal with conflict and what would it look like for you to "fight well"?

6. Practice being present.

Habitual hiding must first be unlearned. We tend to hide so frequently, we don't even know how we are truly feeling. Consider the last challenge or struggle you faced: What were you feeling and why? What was beneath that? Next time, you may remember to stop, take a breath, and slow down to recognize the anxiety underneath your response and even why it has more to do with the past (or fears of the future) than the present. Again, vulnerability is less about stating the fact (though that's a great start) and more about how you are experiencing that fact. For example, perhaps the fact is: *I dropped off my wife at the hospital for a checkup.* Vulnerability is: *I was so anxious about the future that I quickly dropped her off and didn't even give her a hug. I wanted to but I didn't.* This is why people who say they don't have a problem with vulnerability because they are an open book and are direct and honest may not actually be vulnerable. There are layers of vulnerability:

> **FIRST LAYER:** *I lied* (you may settle here thinking you are being vulnerable)
> **SECOND LAYER:** *I lied because I didn't want to look bad* (addressing the why)
> **THIRD LAYER:** *I'm genuinely scared to lose you* (adding how you actually feel)

7. Practice saying the three little words with big power.[14]

In any relational setting, these three words carry powerful vulnerability:

Sorry
Help
Thanks

They are not crazy, revolutionary concepts, but they're not often heard and can be quite difficult for some people to say. However, when the words are uttered in honesty, there seems to be a pause in the atmosphere, in people's hearts. They're that powerful. They can draw us near to others, and they can help others move toward us.

In Korean, the word for mother is 어머니. It's pronounced *Uh-Muh-Nee*. What's fascinating is that this word can be used to refer to anyone who may be in a similar life stage as my mom—a friend's mom, storeowner, or church leader. Koreans frequently use it to bridge the gap for offering greater intimacy with others. This is the power of words. Words have the power to offer belonging.

Which word is the most challenging for you to say—*sorry*, *help*, or *thanks*?

TMI

Do you know anyone who has the tendency to overshare or over-explain themselves? Perhaps that's happened and you've thought to yourself, *TMI* (too much information). My wife would say that's usually a trauma or anxiety response coming from being blamed or misunderstood. Another reason for oversharing is a longing for connection, intimacy, and belonging. But in doing this people fail to realize "it often results in disconnection, distrust, and disengagement."[15] There is often an inability to discern the right context, people, timing, and amount of relational trust. If that is you, one helpful question to ask yourself is: *Why* am I sharing this?

Vulnerability is not recklessness. I would not tell my two young daughters, in the name of being "authentic and vulnerable," all of our marriage's struggles or burden them with our family's needs. That would be foolish of me. Some of my friends bring their intensity, depth, and "authentic vulnerable self" into every conversation and reject light and casual conversation as shallow and superficial. This is also foolish. Relational wisdom requires appropriate vulnerability and not some false expectation that everyone must hold all of me at all times.

8. Find safe people.

How do you know who's safe and who's not? When connecting through vulnerability, always go slow and start small: share something mildly personal and see how they respond. Friends won't shame you or gossip and are great at listening and reciprocating. It can seem nearly impossible to find people who can handle being vulnerable, but modeling it and even talking about it will inspire you and build your courage. Find someone to meet with you this week or next to begin slowly listening to and sharing with. Good therapists, spiritual directors, and pastors are also options. Support groups are great because the environment itself says, *Hey, we are all in this together.* Find someone you can begin to exercise your vulnerability muscles with safely.

As I mentioned earlier, Tuesday nights are when our men's group intentionally builds and uses these muscles of vulnerability. This is the place I've felt safest, so I prioritized it, recognized chemistry with others in the group, and I've practiced staying present when emotion comes. Everyone in our group has committed to these things, which makes going deeper possible. Vulnerability is not easy, but we lean into it instead of fighting or fleeing it, which has brought deeper connection, intimacy, and belonging. Any struggle—marriage, parenting, money, injustices, power differences, and losses (including loss of personal control over these things)—we can grieve together. Whether death, unemployment, addictions, or deep griefs over our parents and children, we're held by people who care, and we're reminded of our calling to be faithful husbands, fathers, and sons.

We experience freedom when things in the dark come to light. They lose their power. We see ourselves becoming people of integrity and honesty. Vulnerability also increases our personal accountability and challenges us to take greater responsibility for our actions. Ultimately, vulnerability increases our belonging because we are now all holding the real versions of one another.

Our next practice is controversial. But of course, that's often a measure of its importance. Let's take a look.

Vulnerability Reflection

- When you think of God, what are the first three attributes that come to mind? Don't give your Sunday Christian answer. Give the first three attributes that immediately come to your mind. (I use this exercise in workshops to identify how you primarily think about God. This shapes your vulnerability journey with God.)
- Warm-up questions to get you going:
  - What do you like about yourself?
  - What's the harshest comment you've ever received and why?
  - Describe the most humiliating thing you've experienced.
  - Which cultural challenge to vulnerability affects you the most and why?
  - Which Christian challenge to vulnerability affects you the most and why?
- Take a moment to examine your life. Is there something you are intentionally hiding? Name it here. Then ask yourself why.
- What safe people can you contact to begin the process?

Chapter 6

Priority #4: Empathy

SUPPORTING OTHERS WELL IN A

SELF-ABSORBED WORLD

I t was May 27, 2018.

There was a common traffic jam on the California freeway. I brought our car to a full stop, but a person behind us wasn't paying attention. Their car slammed into my car at seventy miles per hour, rear-ending us on our way to church. The trunk of our 2003 Toyota Matrix was crushed immediately, both rear tires popped on impact, our side windows shattered, and all four doors became jammed. In our confusion, Nina and I looked at each other to confirm we were still alive and then turned to our two girls.

As a new father familiar with the dangers of Silicon Valley traffic, being rear-ended was one of my greatest fears. My two girls were under three at the time, and when my wife and I turned around, we couldn't easily tell if they were okay due to their rear-facing car seats. We scrambled out of our broken side windows—both of us losing our sandals in the process, cars still driving by—but we had forgotten everything except rescuing our girls. Bare feet stepping on shattered glass, we had one mission: open the jammed doors and get our girls out. At this point, we still couldn't tell if they were okay.

The doors weren't budging and we couldn't find our cell phones, so I waved my hands, yelling for help. A car slowed and rolled down the window, but the passenger only held up a phone to record me. Then another one, and another. I couldn't process it. I tried desperately to make eye contact, begging someone to call 911. But each one continued on, phones still pointing our way.

I've never felt so abandoned. I deeply felt the cry, *Does anyone hear me, see me?*

Soon, one car and then another stopped. One driver came out to direct traffic, another called 911, and a tall, muscular, middle-aged father helped get our girls out. "I'm late for my son's baseball game," he said. "But as a father myself, I understand what you are going through. I'm going to stay and help as much as I can."

"Thank you," I said, nearly breaking down.

"I got you. We're gonna get your kids out. Don't worry."

Then he took out a baseball bat from his trunk to break through the remaining windows. He looked like a superhero. Actually, he was one.

We weren't alone anymore.

We got the girls out and they were okay. We all survived the accident but it took us years to fully recover. And I share all this because of the two different ways people responded to our pain and suffering that day: one of distance and one of closeness, or empathy. Empathy is moving toward the other person, and it creates intimacy and belonging. *Empathy is doing your best to understand people.* It's a posture of choosing to listen to another instead of assuming you know where they're coming from. With empathy, we are able to not only recognize but identify with and even feel the feelings and needs of others. Therefore, empathy is the ability to understand, experience, and respond to the other person appropriately.

We all come into the world in the most vulnerable position. And every time our vulnerability is not met with empathy, we start hiding out of self-protection. This is why empathy must follow vulnerability in our journey of belonging.

Brené Brown, well-known author and research professor at the University of Houston, said it like this: "Empathy has no script. There is no right way or wrong way to do it. It's simply listening, holding space, withholding judgment, emotionally connecting, and communicating that incredibly healing message of 'You're not alone.'"[1] It means that you hear and see me. Empathy offers *togetherness.*

But sadly, you've probably noticed, like I did during my accident, that empathy is not common. Actually, we are facing an empathy deficit. Professors, psychologists, and empathy researchers have all observed a steep decline in empathy in our world today. We lack concern for others when they are in deep pain, and in everyday conversations, we have an argumentative posture about the cruelty we see all around the world.[2] Even in our workplace, "68 percent of CEOs say they fear they will be less respected if they show empathy."[3] What's been your experience in your workplace? Is it common to have regular check-ins for your well-being? Maybe, maybe not.

Even in the church, we believe a great pastor-leader is someone strong, aggressive, and "charismatic." This kind of belief makes it fertile ground for narcissistic leaders to be in demand and empathy traits to be cast out as weakness. Chuck DeGroat is a seminary professor and counselor who trains and works with numerous pastors and leaders around the nation. In his book *When Narcissism Comes to Church*, he reflects, "In my lifetime, the classic image of the devoted parish pastor who could be trusted to rightly preach the word, diligently care for souls, and wisely lead the church has shifted dramatically."[4]

And for those who generally live in their own headspace, it's always a challenge to be emotionally supportive. Just thinking about the implications of these two words can confuse and scare people. Even for those who are more naturally empathetic, empathy that deepens healthy belonging (as you will see) is another matter.

Thankfully, empathy is a skill that we can develop! That's what the second half of this chapter will be about. But before we get to the practical steps, let me first introduce you to the four enemies of empathy that stand in our way of greater belonging in our climate today. As we value speed, efficiency, and data more and more, these enemies of empathy have become stronger than ever.

ENEMIES OF EMPATHY

Indifference

Humans throughout history had access to mainly local news. There was no such thing as the internet. (I know! Can you believe that?) For anything that was happening far away, it took months for that news to travel to your area. And by the time you received it, who knew what the current state of things was? Globalization has given our society the gift to communicate and share resources and information in a way that's never been done before. At the same time, we now have access to terrifying news happening all over the world.

We hear of an earthquake that caused seven hundred deaths, then a friend's cancer diagnosis, then a clip of someone being unjustly tried for a murder—and a hundred more things in less than five minutes. The *Oxford English Dictionary* named *doom-scrolling*, this tendency to continue to scroll through bad news, as a word of the year in 2020. One could argue this is due to all of us being stuck at home during the pandemic in 2020, but many of us do this every day, filling our minds with such tragedies that each one could take weeks, even months to process, which constantly overwhelms our finite human souls with what only God can handle. Clearly, there needs to be more wisdom and discernment applied here.

Now please hear me. I'm not saying we should close our eyes and not care about the world. But some of us at certain times may need to be more careful about preserving our hearts by eliminating what we have no business knowing, especially if there's nothing we can do about it. There's much that's inspiring and positive in our feeds, and, of course, we ought to pray and lean in where we can. But this unfiltered news feed has caused fatigue, desensitization, and dullness to our own and others' pain.

We can too easily become indifferent. So we need to guard against this. When thinking back to our accident, I've come to realize that many of us have become numb to people's pain and don't even realize it. Information overload has made many of us indifferent.

Impatience

Not long ago, my wife, Nina, and I had an argument. An hour after I got to work, this text popped up on my phone:

> I think when someone expresses anxiety or a need, you get overwhelmed because you think it's your responsibility to put the fire out. I appreciate that but I don't need you to do that right now. I'm a grown adult, I will figure it out. I just need you to listen and give reassurance as a friend would. So I don't feel alone.

Almost a decade into our marriage, I still try to fix and find solutions instead of actually listening and comforting my wife.

Then a few minutes later, I got another text from Nina:

> Just sit with me as I go through it and it will pass.

I knew she was right. People often don't need solutions. They just need a friend to be there. And if she wanted solutions, she would have asked for that. She wanted to know she wasn't alone, and that I cared and was with her. But if I'm being honest, I like quick fixes because empathy is time-consuming, pain-inducing, and exhausting. You have to use your mental and emotional energy, and many times I'm too selfish to care that deeply for others. I hate "wasting" time—but empathy requires time. Technological advances and microwaveable culture have made me irritated and uneasy about anything that's slow. Like empathy. And deep relationships.

Through her emotional honesty, my amazing, insightful wife helped me come to this painful realization: my impatience brought a lack of empathy in my life and caused me to be alone. Who wants to build a meaningful relationship with someone who has no real interest in their needs? How often do I prefer results over people? Some of us, maybe especially men, need to ask these painful questions.

Insecurity

Whether someone is sharing a huge win or a huge mistake in their lives, it stirs up all sorts of thoughts and emotions.

Think back to the story of Saul and David. Scripture tells us:

> When the men were returning home after David had killed the Philistine, the women came out from all the towns of Israel to meet King Saul with singing and dancing, with joyful songs and with timbrels and lyres. As they danced, they sang: "Saul has slain his thousands, and David his tens of thousands." Saul was very angry; this refrain displeased him greatly. "They have credited David with tens of thousands," he thought, "but me with only thousands. What more can he get but the kingdom?" And from that time on Saul kept a close eye on David. (1 Samuel 18:6–9 NIV)

I would think as a warrior, to slay thousands is an incredible feat (and yes, barbaric). But as soon as Saul's body count was compared to David's, insecurity kicked in. Had Saul not been so insecure, he and David might have had a close relationship. Insecurity can also make us arrogant:

> To some who were confident of their own righteousness and looked down on everyone else, Jesus told this parable: "Two men went up to the temple to pray, one a Pharisee and the other a

tax collector. The Pharisee stood by himself and prayed: 'God, I thank you that I am not like other people—robbers, evildoers, adulterers—or even like this tax collector.'" (Luke 18:9–11 NIV)

We cannot empathize with other people's sufferings, failures, and mistakes when pride puts distance between us. We miss the invitation from Paul in Philippians: "Do nothing from selfish ambition or conceit, but in humility count others more significant than yourselves" (2:3).

Insecurity makes us compare ourselves with others and we lose the ability to see them. We are so concerned about not measuring up or proving we're superior that everyone else takes a back seat. In the process, we lose ourselves, and our fears rule us.

When our insecurity triggers comparison, any real support or celebration of others is nullified. We pull away. Maybe we need to take a break from seeing everyone's feed of "highlight reels."

Ignorance

The last enemy of empathy may be the biggest: biblical ignorance. Imagine you've just lost your job or have been injured. At the same time, a close friend has a miscarriage or loses someone they love. Some might think, *God must be punishing us for our sins.* Sadly that's a common thought, but it lacks knowledge of God's character.

Think of Job's famous three friends. When they saw Job's suffering, they were convinced that Job was suffering due to his sins. They were narrow-minded in the sense that they had only one reasonable conclusion for his suffering—and in the process misrepresented God. God eventually stepped in and corrected their inaccurate thinking—"My anger burns against you and against your two friends, for you have not spoken of me what is right, as my servant Job has" (Job 42:7)—but Job's story reveals how bad theology can prevent genuine care, love, and support. Sound theology matters, friends. We've got to be constant learners of the Bible.

Growing up, I thought of empathy as a cousin of vulnerability in the sense that empathy looked weak and didn't seem to hold enough truth. It had too much emotion and could even result in agreeing with or approving too much of the person's experience and felt-reality rather than with what the Bible says. This led to my passion for Jesus directly translating to rebuking and correcting others. I believed my empathy would get in the way of their journey to holiness and enable their behaviors. When other Christians talked about love and empathy, I judged them as young or immature in their faith and believed that genuine Christianity involves only "proclaiming the truth in this godless world."

I may have missed the memo from Paul, who said, "Praise be to the God and Father of our Lord Jesus Christ, the Father of compassion and the God of all comfort, who comforts us in all our troubles, so that we can comfort those in any trouble with the comfort we ourselves receive from God" (2 Corinthians 1:3–4 NIV).

Ignorance leads to insensitivity or tone-deafness. We become out of touch, unaware, careless, even cruel to social cues and nuances of life. It's telling your friend you got a huge raise when he just shared about losing his job. It's talking to a group of stay-at-home moms and saying how easy they have it compared to working moms. It's telling an anxious person to just get over it and be more brave. It's not reaching out to your coworkers who are struggling with tensions, whether it be financial, racial, or health-related. It's really the inability to "read the room."[5] Human relationships need wisdom, nuance, and sensitivity, and tone-deafness causes more pain and tension.

There's a lot of ignorance that steals deeper empathy. And all these enemies of empathy bring distance, not closeness. In fact, I recently came across another ignorant idea that hinders belonging in Christian community.

IS EMPATHY SINFUL?

As a pastor, I believe I can always lean on the Christian faith to help me grow in empathy. So I was caught off-guard when I was researching this chapter and did what every great scholar does. I googled my topic: "Christianity and empathy."

What I found on the very first page shocked me: "The Sin of Empathy." *Huh?*

Now, this wasn't some random article. This was on the first page of results, from a popular Christian blog. This and other sites like it warn that empathy can make us lose the ability to discern "truth vs. feelings." They argue we can end up agreeing with the other person's feelings and/or sins by fusing with them. In other words, *enmeshment*.

Surprising? I thought so. But as you can see, there is much confusion around what empathy is and what our proper response and posture should be. Over the years, I've seen Christians all over the map on this topic and what I've found very helpful is something I call "The Empathy Scale."

In this empathy scale, there are two forces on opposite sides, each constantly pulling us to its side. The two forces are *individuality* and *togetherness*. Both aren't bad things in and of themselves. But when individuality alone is emphasized, the scale will move toward the left (more common in the West) and find its place in indifference or sympathy. When togetherness alone is emphasized, the scale will move toward the right (more common in the East) and find its place in acceptance or enmeshment.[6]

When it's balanced, we achieve *empathy*.

We already discussed in the beginning how indifference works. But there's another way that's particularly troubling because it masquerades as being "biblical."

Recently, a woman came up after one of my sermons to talk to me about her close relative who, as an evangelist-pastor, bases his ministry on one verse: "But Jehu the son of Hanani the seer went out to meet him and said to King Jehoshaphat, 'Should you help the wicked and love those who hate the LORD? Because of this, wrath has gone out against you from the LORD'" (2 Chronicles 19:2). His belief is that Christians aren't to love those who "hate the Lord" because God's wrath will come upon us and that our main job is to preach judgment against the wicked.

Besides the fact that the verse was taken out of context, the entire Bible is about God's great love and mercy toward all of us who have rebelled and resisted Him. How many Christians have sadly taken the posture of anger, judgment, and an "us versus them" attitude? I write this not to condemn them, but to ask why. I have compassion for them because I have done similar things. For a time, I thought my interpretation and theology were right, and that other Christians had missed the deeper point of the Bible. Often, our very posture is that of indifference. Yet when I consider how Jesus corrected so many of our misunderstandings about God, I remember we all need His mercy and grace.

Though we know there is a difference, we often confuse sympathy with empathy. Sympathy says, *Oh, I feel sorry for you.* It reserves its distance. Empathy, on the other hand, is doing our best to actually feel what the other person is feeling, and thereby creating closeness. Scot McKnight said, "Empathic persons enter into the feelings of others for the sake of support, relief and healing."[7]

On the other side of empathy, we have *unqualified acceptance*. This is when, in our empathy, we affirm and accept all feelings, but reserve approval of some actions and decisions. This can get complicated. Sometimes out of fear of looking unloving, we agree with everything someone is saying or doing. This is another misunderstanding of empathy. Empathy doesn't mean accepting everything about the other person's thoughts and choices.

Recently, I met with a woman (let's call her Jen) who came from a spiritually and emotionally abusive church. As she was processing the pain, she had a deep desire to return in order to begin the process of reconciliation, even though the leadership of the church admitted to zero fault. I empathized with her pain and confusion by saying, "I'm so sorry that you had to go through this, and our church will do everything we can to walk with you and get you the help you need to heal, but going back to talk to their leadership right now might not be the best step." I had to be ever so careful because my main job was to listen, comfort, and support Jen, not to teach or even guide her. But it's not pastoral, and is ultimately unhelpful, to merely agree with everything.

There is a temptation, in the name of empathy, to resist any kind of guidance and direction for life change. We can weaponize empathy with the claim "you're not showing me enough empathy" and reject truth and sound wisdom. Our impulse for transformation is the Spirit of God, not how much the conversation was padded with empathy (more on this in the final practice, next chapter).

We must also be careful not to move so far into another's feelings and emotions we end up confusing what's what and whose is whose. Christian love does not say "you must take on all that they feel and become just like them." Enmeshment is another empathy miss. True empathy is moving into the emotion and still keeping the focus on *them*. We all know people who are incredibly emotive, and in their empathy, they end up making it about themselves. The focus goes to *their* pain and emotional distress and the attention shifts away from the other person.

Or they get so wrapped up in their empathetic engagement that they experience the other person's stress and pain for days and weeks to come. If not careful, first responders and therapists like my wife can experience what we call *vicarious trauma*.

Bottom line, the ability to offer proper empathy requires *differentiation*. Pastor and author Steve Cuss, borrowing wisdom from family systems theory sages like Murray Bowen and Edwin Friedman, said, "Differentiation [is attaining] clarity on where you end and the 'other' begins. The two opposites are indifference and enmeshment. Healthy space, clarity of values, while staying connected to another. Differentiated people can manage their reactivity and become a non-anxious presence."[8]

Too much individuality leads us to become indifferent and disconnected, while too much togetherness leads us to become enmeshed and entangled.

Differentiation is only possible when in our journey of love, care, and empathy, we have also done enough boundary work. Protecting my boundaries is not an act of selfishness (though I heard that a lot growing up) but a way to protect and serve others well. I will give some actionable steps for this at the end of the chapter. For now, we need to recognize that true empathy isn't sinful.

Let's look at an example in the Bible of empathy done right.

JOB'S FRIENDS

Job's friends are often made out to be bad examples of friendship and empathy in the midst of suffering. And while they did miss the mark on all sorts of things, they also did some things right, especially in the first seven days:

> Now when Job's three friends heard of all this evil that had come upon him, they came each from his own place, Eliphaz the Temanite, Bildad the Shuhite, and Zophar the Naamathite. They made an appointment together to come to show him sympathy and comfort him. And when they saw him from a distance, they did not recognize him. And they raised their voices and wept, and they tore their robes and sprinkled dust on their heads toward heaven. And they sat with him on the ground seven days and seven nights, and no one spoke a word to him, for they saw that his suffering was very great. (Job 2:11–13)

You can't read this and think, *Oh what terrible friends!* They deliberately talked among themselves to gather together and show empathy in unison. They fully engaged in the grieving process with cries, tears, and the physical acts of tearing their robes and the sprinkling of dust. And most important of all, they sat with Job for *seven days and seven nights* in silence. When my wife is going through and processing difficult things in her life, I have a hard time staying silent for more than fifteen minutes! Regardless of their later failure, this started out as a beautiful picture of empathy.

Suffering isolates us from others as we think, *No one understands what I'm going through. I'm all alone.* But here is the good news. While we are in our most vulnerable state in pain, our bonds are forged through sharing in the hardships of life. And empathy offers the opportunity to strengthen our ties and remind one another that we are in this together. It's unlikely we would name anyone meaningful in our lives who did not walk through some hard times with us.

CELEBRATIVE EMPATHY

Of course, empathy is not only reserved for situations that are incredibly sad.

We tend to associate empathy primarily with others' suffering and pain, but celebrating with those who are celebrating is also a crucial part of empathy and belonging. The apostle Paul wrote, "Rejoice with those who rejoice, and weep with those who weep. Be of the same mind toward one another" (Romans 12:15–16 NKJV). I love that. Empathy is being of the same mind toward one another, which includes both the highs and lows of life.

If empathy is doing our best to understand people, leaning into others' joys and victories is certainly part of that journey. Sadly, King Saul wasn't able to celebrate David's success due to his insecurity. Think back to your birthdays, key accomplishments, and milestones. When folks join in and are genuinely happy for and with you, how does that affect you? When there are both small and big wins in our lives, we long to share our joy with others. And when it is met with genuine cheers, we experience that our joy is their joy.

Celebration both strengthens and reinforces belonging. In the Old Testament, God called for festivals and celebration markers to remind a forgetful Israel that they belonged to Him and one another. Such empathy reminds us we are in this incredible journey together.

EMPATHY IN ACTION

Jesus was the master at showing empathy. There are many times in His ministry when He was moved and filled with compassion toward others (Mark 6:34; Luke 7:13). I believe compassion is *empathy in action*. And I think it's worthwhile to revisit the story where two sisters, Martha and Mary, were experiencing the death of their brother, Lazarus.

Let's return to John 11, where Jesus had arrived after Lazarus's death. John captured this scene beautifully and intentionally:

> "Lord," Martha said to Jesus, "*if you had been here, my brother would not have died.* But I know that even now God will give you whatever you ask." Jesus said to her, "Your brother will rise again" . . . When Mary reached the place where Jesus was and saw him, she fell at his feet and said, "Lord, *if you had been here, my brother would not have died.*" When Jesus saw her weeping, and the Jews who had come along with her also weeping, he was deeply moved in spirit and troubled. "Where have you laid him?" he asked. "Come and see, Lord," they replied. Jesus wept. (vv. 21–23, 32–35 NIV, emphasis added)

Notice how Martha and Mary said the same thing to Jesus. They both experienced the same loss, but Jesus responded differently to each because their needs were different. Martha needed Jesus' words of assurance, while Mary needed His tears. Jesus moved toward them in empathy but in two different ways. Empathy doesn't say, *I'm going to respond the way I like*—empathy searches the hearts of others and responds according to their needs.

God always moves toward us. Jesus' incarnation is a reminder that God comes to us. He chases after us. He seeks us out. We see time and again, Jesus entered into people's pain and offered grace and hope, and not from a distance. As John would say, "the Word became flesh and made his dwelling among us" (John 1:14 NIV).

This is why the author of Hebrews could comfort and encourage us with these words: "For we do not have a high priest who is unable to *empathize*[9] with our weaknesses, but we have one who has been tempted in every way, just as we are—yet he did not sin" (Hebrews 4:15 NIV, emphasis added). Jesus understands our human struggles. Our frustration, struggles, and prayers of desperation are met with empathy, not indifference. And He doesn't just feel sorry for us; He's willing to help us—He carried it to Calvary. So yes, He understands our struggles. But it's so much more than that.

The Bible reminds us that we have the Holy Spirit who is the *Paraclete*—which can be translated as the Comforter, Advocate, Helper, or Counselor—guiding and caring for us (John 14:26). God knows us so well and comforts us according to our needs.

He is so good.

A QUIET CHRISTMAS EVE

Christmas Eve is one of my favorite services at our church. I love the carols, the amazing performances, everyone's colorful sweaters and cheerful greetings. And every year, the retelling of Jesus' birth reminds me that in the midst of a broken world, all is not lost.

Yet if you ever visit my church, I'd also mention another service in our nearby chapel. This service is for those who have lost a loved one or experience pain during the holidays and need a space to reflect, pray, and grieve. It was started by my pastors who had lost their son many years ago. Since then, the "Grief Shared" service has become part of our Christmas Eve services every year.

I attended the year of our family's car accident. That year I found I had no strength to attend the larger Christmas Eve service.

Sensing the Spirit's leading, I slowly (nervously) walked in and sat toward the back. I saw many families, maybe sixty to seventy folks, who I imagined each held deep, unexplainable pain. We wished each other "Merry Christmas" and sang a few songs, and then recited a liturgy proclaiming key truths of the Christian faith in the midst of pain. My pastor's message was on the hope found in the gospel, and nothing felt rushed or agenda-driven. Instead, it felt slow, quiet, and reflective. Toward the end of the service, the pastors asked each family, who wanted to share, to say the name of the person they had lost: father, mother, grandparent, sibling, son, or daughter.

"My precious wife, *Caroline*."
"My dad, *Roger*."
"Our daughter, *Gloria*."
"Uncle *John*."

The holiday season and family gatherings only enhanced the pain for these families. One cannot and should not ignore their absences. My pastors, in their pain and empathy, offered the people a sacred space—that it's okay to cry and not have the energy to smile and say "Merry Christmas." Even at Christmas, we can lament and grieve our loved ones. For those who cannot celebrate the "normal" way on Christmas, you belong here. Although I hadn't lost anyone, I walked away knowing that my story has a place in this community. Empathy's gift is safety. If vulnerability is not met with empathy and safety, we will hide even more, until we cannot be found.

We will experience all types of loss in our lifetime—health, friends, dreams, money, relationships, childhood, jobs, and family members—we can't avoid it. Every loss will feel like being dropped off in the middle of a foreign country—feeling directionless, frustrated, overwhelmed, or alone. We ask ourselves: *Where am I? Where is my place? Where do I go from here?*

We can try to run away from pain but eventually unresolved grief will find us through constant irritability, numbness, or depression. Instead of living our lives on autopilot, dealing with grief will enlarge our capacity to sit with pain, find healing, and become more understanding of other people whose lives are also filled with many losses. I can tell you firsthand that I've avoided difficult emotions most of my life, and learning to name and process my grief has been a turning point in my empathy journey.[10]

If pain and brokenness is our human experience until Jesus returns and makes all things new, much of doing life with others is learning to do "grief shared."

Here is our fourth belonging icon: empathy.

We care. We celebrate. We lean in.

We meet them where they are.

And we do our best to see and understand from their perspective.

HOW TO BE BETTER WITH EMPATHY: NINE SKILLS TO PRACTICE

The good news is that even if you aren't a naturally empathetic person, there is hope. Thankfully it's a skill that we can work on. I've learned over the years not to get overwhelmed here. Choose one area of empathy to grow in, practice it, come back and revisit, and work on another. Take your time.

1. Ask the question we don't want to ask.

If you'd like to know more about yourself, the best (and possibly scariest) question to ask others is this: "How do you experience me?"

I may or may not have heard these words when asking that question:

You come off as aggressive and arrogant.
You care only about your own success and work.
You don't seem to have much awareness about other people because you are too self-focused.
You seem uncomfortable and unresponsive when I bring up emotional pain.

No matter where you are, this question will be helpful because you are learning how you really engage in empathy.

2. Remember your Luke 18:13 moment(s).

Luke wrote, "To some who were confident of their own righteousness and looked down on everyone else, Jesus told this parable" (Luke 18:9 NIV). In the parable, the Pharisee bragged about how amazing he was while the tax collector stood at a distance recognizing his brokenness and crying out. Verse 13 says, "He would not even look up to heaven, but beat his breast and said, 'God, have mercy on me, a sinner.'" The more we understand the depths of our sins and the grace given to us, the more empathy and compassion we will have for others. When we are honest about where we've come from and who we are, we begin to slowly heal from indifference, impatience, insecurity, and ignorance, and our hearts become tender with how people are struggling and carrying their pain.

It really comes down to receiving Christ's love in every part of our lives. Jesus said, "Just as I have loved you, you also are to love one another" (John 13:34). In other words, if our core identity isn't formed on the love of Christ, it's hard to love others well. When we come from a deep place where we know and experience that we are fully loved by God, our insecurities, fears, and selfishness take a back seat and we are able to lean into compassion and empathy toward others.

3. Celebrate both big and small wins.

We are great at celebrating big moments in life such as weddings, graduations, birthdays, and anniversaries. But we aren't so great at smaller celebrations. I would argue many frequent smaller celebrations bring greater empathy and belonging than these once-a-year festivities. My friend recently had a long week due to some significant interpersonal issues at work, so a few of the guys got together late at night with some drinks and laughter to celebrate his finishing the hard week.

4. Delight in others.

As we dance, sing, drink, hug, eat, and share important moments of God's goodness in our lives, we experience belonging.

We know from neuroscience these activities release happy chemicals in our brains that reduce stress and offer connection. Cynicism and a pessimistic outlook on life are not signs of wisdom and maturity. We have much to celebrate and be thankful for. Let us laugh and be silly with one another, even in celebrating the small things.

Recently, I've been exhausted from writing this book. As I'm finishing this chapter, my buddy Jeff sent me a card saying, "You've got this! Finish strong!" with a gift card to my favorite local coffee shop where I write every day. It's been a long, lonely journey writing this book on belonging (oh, the irony!), but I felt my friend's presence, love, and support.

5. Learn their full story.

I've heard it said: "Everyone is fighting a battle you don't know about. Be kind always." What if the person who cut you off on the road is actually driving toward a family emergency? What if the person is dealing with mental health issues?

Leading with questions and curiosity instead of assumptions and statements goes a long way. During the height of anti-Asian hate crimes and racial tensions, I shared with my group my pain and frustration. I still remember this moment. One of the guys said, "I'm really new to this. Could you tell me more about AAPI [Asian Americans and Pacific Islanders]? What are some books you recommend? Can I ask you some personal questions to understand where you are coming from? I honestly don't understand it all."

This meant the world to me.

Understanding gives greater space for grace.

We must read and learn widely.

And for those who are close to us, watch out for the closeness-confirmation bias,[11] where we unconsciously tune them out since we already know what they will think and say. Instead of being involved in people's evolving stories, we make assumptions that hinder us in honoring how they may have changed. If you hear words like "that's not what I said" or "you are not listening" often from your close friends, it's time to evaluate your posture. Are you operating out of curiosity or out of closeness-confirmation bias?

6. Listen well and validate.

Communication is so much more than words; in fact, it may be more nonverbal than verbal. Facial expressions, tone of voice, body posture, gestures, and physical distance all matter.

When conversing:

- Pay attention
- Make eye contact
- Ask pertinent questions
- Don't interrupt

I know this sounds like Communication 101, but we all get this wrong at times and need to work at it to improve. Dallas Willard famously said, "The first act of love is always the giving of attention."[12] Asking "what's something you are looking forward to this upcoming year?" and making eye contact and being attentive to their answer offers an opportunity to bond and show empathy. Good listening helps to fight against any shame and fear of judgment in vulnerability.

I mentioned Gottman's "Bids for Connection" in the last chapter. Paying attention and recognizing other people's bids can be really helpful.[13] Validation in listening is something I've learned more recently and have found valuable in my own journey of empathy.[14]

Often when we share, we are longing for someone on the other side to see and support us. Here are some examples of both validating and invalidating responses.

- **VALIDATING RESPONSES:** "Oh, wow, that sounds hard!" "That would also drive me crazy." "You put a lot of work into that." These acknowledge and offer helpful justification for what the person is going through.
- **INVALIDATING RESPONSES:** "You'll be fine." "Just suck it up." "It could be worse." These result in minimizing and dismissing the other person's situation and emotions.

As Jesus followers, we must also listen to the Spirit's leading. We do this because God is already at work in this individual and He knows best. So we pray: *Jesus, help me to notice and obey the nudging of the Holy Spirit in this particular situation.*

7. Learn and lean into their personality and preferences.

I have found Gary Chapman's book *The Five Love Languages* to be practical and helpful. The five "love languages" he describes are *physical touch, quality time, gifts, words of affirmation,* and *acts of service.* The point is that all of us receive and give love (and empathy) differently.

For example, I love receiving words of affirmation. When I'm not doing well, a few words of encouragement can bring me back to life. Especially when the words of affirmation are specific and nuanced, I feel seen and loved because that means the person cared enough to observe and take interest in my life.

Humans are much more complex than simply where they fall on the introvert-extrovert scale. Who we are is also defined by how we see and interact with the world (whether primarily from the head, heart, or gut), how we take in information, what our core fears and communication styles are, and so much more. When there is a greater awareness of our complex selves, our ability to lean in with others is much stronger, and we can be more thoughtful and honoring of the other person. The Myers-Briggs Temperament Indicator, the Enneagram, and the Big Five Personality Traits can be helpful assessments for building your awareness.

8. Give better options.

Generally, we mean well when we respond by saying: "Let me know if you need anything." However, this puts more responsibility on the recipient by requiring them to both think of their needs and reach out again. I have found it is more thoughtful and helpful to offer several suggestions and let them pick one or two. For example, offer to

- drop off some food this week,
- take their kids out to a park so they can get a small break, or
- gather some friends to talk and laugh together.

This shows that you've done some heavy lifting in thinking through what might be helpful and you are giving them the freedom to choose what would most benefit them.

9. Practice self-differentiation.

This comes down to our ability to identify and separate what is ours from theirs. This skill is needed for those who, in their efforts of empathy, have the tendency to become entangled in the other person's feelings, emotions, and situations. This requires boundary work where we learn and begin to practice not owning someone else's stuff in unhealthy ways (having a "savior complex," severe fatigue, and even burnout). This requires us to take some time for ourselves by journaling or taking a walk to ask, *How am I doing? Is this my stuff or their stuff?*

This reminds me of Paul's letter to the Galatian churches: "Carry each others' burdens [*baros*] . . . for each one should carry their own load [*phortion*]" (6:2–5). On the surface, his words may sound contradictory but notice the two different Greek words that are used here. *Baros* in Greek refers to a heavy burden and weight that requires assistance. *Phortion* is more of a traveler's pack, a load that an individual can carry. Self-differentiation invites us to discern what we are called to be responsible for and what we are called to share and carry together.

I have found that working on one skill at a time is most effective. If we want to master any skill in cooking, musical instruments, or sports, we repeat it until it becomes natural to us. Which of these nine skills does it seem like God is inviting you to practice in this season?

How do you know if you're growing in empathy?

> **HERE IS THE TEST:** People in distress come to you for comfort.
> **WE PRAY:** Jesus, please enlarge my capacity to suffer with others well.

Now it's time to look at the last practice to cultivate belonging: accountability. This anchor triggers all sorts of emotions for people, and generally most are negative. But I believe it doesn't have to be, and though it can be the most dangerous and difficult practice, when done right, it offers belonging, community, and transformation in a deeper way than most anything else can.

Empathy Reflection

Let's start with some awareness!

- Ask your peers to give you feedback on your overall listening skills.
  - "Hey, on a scale from 1 to 10, how would you rate my listening skills?"
  - Then, "What can I do to be a better listener?"
- Ask those who are regularly around you: "How do you experience me?" What are you learning about yourself from their answers?
- Is there anyone in your journey of belonging that needs your support or celebration? If so, how would you go about doing that well in empathy?
- What tools are you using to better understand another person? What's been helpful for you?
- On the empathy scale spectrum, where do you usually find yourself?

Chapter 7

Practice #5:
Accountability

THE NECESSARY ROAD TO CHRISTLIKENESS

Have you ever totaled a car? I have—three times. In the miserable winter storms of Boston. I hated the cold and my insurance company hated me even more. It was time to move on. So I applied for a full-time ministry position all the way across the country to get away from Boston. (You may be thinking this is not a spiritual way to make this kind of decision. And yes, you are right. It was just too *cold*.) I still remember the phone call saying they would love to have me fill the position. I couldn't believe it. I was excited and ready to meet my new spiritual family.

Fast-forward to my first day of work. I remember my supervising elder asking if he could have a private chat with me after the worship service. He started the conversation by saying, "I wanted to remind you of a few things before you get started here."

I thought to myself: *Great! Would love to get some wisdom for sure!*

Then I heard words I will never forget: "David, you are just a hired employee and you will never be a part of our church family."

What did he say? I couldn't believe it.

He then paused and came up close to my face. His aggressive, angry tone was unmistakable.

"Remember that. I can kick you out at any time if you screw up. So *don't screw it up*."

I felt like I'd just been gut-punched and left gasping for air. But I understood, loud and clear. He wanted to make sure that I knew he was a powerful boss and would put me in my place. He wanted to remind me that he was watching and that he would hold me accountable.

There is clearly a way accountability can increase belonging and intimacy, and a way where it does not. Quite often, even if it isn't as harsh as this, in Christian contexts, accountability can make people feel more like an outsider than truly supported. If he had said something like "I'd love to come alongside you to help you thrive and serve God's people faithfully. Please let me know how I can support you in this transition," then I would have felt responsible and far more energized to actually try. But apparently, this wasn't the culture I was stepping into.

When there is no genuine care for the other in accountability, we experience relational separation. I've seen the extreme opposite, especially in hierarchical contexts where people are put on pedestals out of reverence and respect, and accountability is met with a strong resistance. The leaders operate as though they are unique and untouchable.

Here is what I've commonly seen regarding accountability:

- Accountability causes *distance* when others are *disregarded*.
- Accountability causes *resistance* when others are *elevated*.

But when done right:

- Accountability causes *connection* when others are *valued.*

Therefore, accountability is not the unfolding of our own agenda in others. True accountability is helping one another become all that God is inviting us to be, in love. Remember, you have earned trust if you have lived out the first four practices of belonging: *priority, chemistry, vulnerability,* and *empathy.* These show that you deeply care and long to do life with others in transformative ways. This is why the order is so important.

Yet, even after becoming skilled in those areas, accountability is often easier said than done.

MY BROTHER DID IT

Poor Jon, my brother, took the brunt of my selfishness growing up. I blamed him for everything, including my own mistakes. I took advantage of our six-year age gap. I never covered for him because I lived for my own well-being. My parents would ask, "Who broke this jar?"

My answer was automatic: "Jon did it!"

"Who didn't clean up this mess?" "Jon!"

I know. God is still doing a ton of work in my life.

And this has been happening from the beginning of time. Remember Adam and Eve? Instead of taking responsibility and covering for each other, they blamed and accused: Adam blamed God and Eve, saying, "The woman you put here with me." Eve said, "The serpent deceived me" (Genesis 3:12–13).

Later, Cain murdered Abel and encountered this question from

God: "Where is your brother Abel?" Cain replied, "I don't know." Denial. Then this: "Am I my brother's keeper?" (Genesis 4:9).

And it's not solely them. We also say, "Am I so-and-so's keeper? Isn't that a codependent relationship? What does that person's well-being have to do with me? It's not my responsibility."

I'm not talking about unhealthy, boundary-less, codependent relationships. What God is talking about is this: to love and care for one another.

We have the tendency not to take responsibility for the welfare of others. We don't experience meaningful belonging because we refuse to serve, protect, and fight for one another. We watch from a distance as others struggle and we let them self-destruct. There's a different way to respect people and experience what "all in" means with someone. But it requires the kind of friendship that says we can't do this life alone and we will help each other become all that God longs for us to be. What accountability means is supporting each other to live in alignment with God's invitation for our lives. While we cannot in our own power transform anyone, by God's Spirit we can remind those we share true connection with that Jesus is our ultimate model, both His life and teachings.

ACCOUNTABILITY LANDMINES

What comes to mind when you hear the word *accountability*?

Don't tell me what I should or shouldn't do.
Don't tell me how I should spend my hard-earned money.
Don't tell me how I should parent.

In our highly individualistic, privacy-first culture, account-ability can sound archaic. Aren't we supposed to mind our own business? Aren't we free to make our own choices without judgment? This makes it difficult to speak into someone's situation.

Thoughts of "accountability group" meetings can be triggering, people sharing the same "minor" sins every week, and the group telling each person to "do better" each time. It so often falls into legalism and the emphasis is on the sins dodged that week. And if we say we don't sin, self-righteousness can kick in instead of the usual shame and guilt.

Maybe you think, *I don't need accountability.* Some say account-ability is anti-Jesus. They believe we are fully forgiven and there is no more condemnation for those who are in Christ Jesus. Therefore, the focus should not be on our sins, but on Jesus. Besides, don't we need more positivity in this culture of cynicism?

Or perhaps you've witnessed how accountability can lead to church abuse. Sadly, this is far too common. In the name of accountability, all sorts of damage has been done. By the way, forced accountability is what we call *abuse.* We've seen how people use "accountability" to control and manipulate. Some Christians might force you to share things you aren't ready to share, or in God's name and authority restrict you from doing things without their permission. I've counseled many individuals who had a pastor or leader tell them they needed their approval to date someone, apply to schools and jobs, and even move to another city.

You may also argue, Shouldn't we only be accountable to God? This is a half-truth, since God also speaks through others. While we must not forget that Jesus is our Lord and King and that each one of us "will give an account of himself to God" (Romans 14:12),

God's rule and reign also comes through the placement of leaders in our lives (Romans 13).

A well-known pastor who was eventually removed for his abusive power and control shunned accountability by saying, "I don't listen to other pastors who have smaller congregations than me." Pride always finds excuses for our behavior.

Other excuses I've heard include that we shouldn't judge others, which is another half-truth (Matthew 7:1–5 says we should judge *rightly*, not judge *never*). People are also often afraid of hurting others' feelings. This one, I deeply empathize with. In our highly sensitive culture, it can seem like we're risking the relationship to assert the need for accountability. But we can't let fear dominate our relationships and expect to find belonging.

In our ever increasing post-Christian context, the source of authority is constantly being questioned and challenged. From a low view of Scripture to suspicion toward institutions and its leadership, and a redefinition of truth as personal experience over objective reality, we must answer yet again Pilate's comment to Jesus: "What is truth?" (John 18:38).

Whew. There are so many hurdles that make accountability much more difficult. One wrong step (whether you know it or not) can trigger a hidden landmine that can hurt you and others in the process. Pastor and author Tim Keller wrote, "Everyone says they want community and friendship. But mention accountability or commitment to people and they run the other way."[1] Accountability is hard work. And it's becoming more rare. The Barna Group surveyed Christians involved in church and found that only 5 percent had some form of accountability, primarily through their small groups.[2]

Yet interestingly, some might say we are getting better at accountability. Typically, these are the folks who love church discipline. They think, *We need more of this!* They're saddened that the current Christian culture is too "lovey-dovey" and has compromised with the world and lost its saltiness. They think we are not harsh enough and need to rebuke people more to course-correct and wake up.

Sadly, while there's some truth there, this isn't that far from the cancel-culture folks.

JUST ONE STRIKE

At our church's newcomers class and luncheon, we offer a chance to get to know our community and welcome any questions people might have. After many years, I noticed the questions have changed. I honestly don't remember hearing questions about accountability until a few years ago. Now, some form of one of these is asked almost every time:

How are your elders/board members selected?
Who keeps the senior leadership accountable and how is this done?
Are there enough checks and balances to prevent abuse of power in the church?

The questions should have been asked long ago, but I'm glad they're finally being asked now. Historically, people with power have had far too much authority, and the ability to abuse the system for gain has run rampant. We know far too many who have been deeply wounded by the very folks who were supposed to protect and care for them. This is not okay, and leaders must take responsibility for their actions.

Nowadays, accountability is sometimes handled via "cancel culture," and even the most powerful get held accountable for their actions, which wasn't the case for most of history. However, the problem is that just one wrong word or act, even if it happened long ago, can be enough to give someone the boot. The court of public opinion doesn't know "three strikes and you're out." Often, just one strike is enough. This ruthlessness makes culture more afraid and ironically less safe. Breaking a law once is more than enough to get you removed or thrown in jail. This means there isn't much space for nuanced conversations. Even when things that are taken out of context and shared on any online platform, an online jury can and will make final decisions for people's futures based on faulty or incomplete information.

We are deeply aware that no one can be defined by one action for the rest of their lives because as followers of Jesus, we are people of *second chances*. Christian faith is built upon healing, forgiveness, grace, and redemption. And yet we are usually too patient with our own sins and too impatient with others'.

Clearly, accountability is incredibly delicate and hard to get right. What we need to know is whether it's even possible to hold grace and truth together anymore. Is anyone doing that well?

ONE PERSON DID IT PERFECTLY!

John wrote, "The Word became flesh and made his dwelling among us. We have seen his glory, the glory of the one and only Son, who came from the Father, *full of grace and truth*" (John 1:14 NIV, emphasis added).

We see a perfect example of this with Jesus and the woman caught in adultery.[3] While the crowd argued to stone this woman, Jesus masterfully said, "Let any one of you who is without sin be the first to throw a stone at her" (John 8:7 NIV). When everyone left, Jesus offered what I see as such beautiful accountability. He offered both grace—"Then neither do I condemn you"—and truth—"Go now and leave your life of sin" (John 8:11 NIV).

Tim Keller suggests that "'truth' without grace is not really truth and 'grace' without truth is not really grace."[4] But we've all met people who emphasize one over the other. Pastor and professor Kevin DeYoung is also helpful and worth quoting at length:

> Grace people without truth are pleasant to be around, but we wonder if they really like us or if they are just trying to be liked. . . . They accept us for who we are, but they never help us become who we should be. And then there are truth people. Truth people are easy to admire. They have convictions and principles. They believe in right and wrong. . . . But without grace, telling the truth can become an excuse for belligerence. Truth people without grace are loyal to their cause, but we wonder if they are really loyal to us. . . .
>
> If you are a grace person you are most concerned about being loved. If you are a truth person you are most concerned about being right even if it means being unloved. Both have their dangers. Something is wrong if everyone hates you, and something is probably just as wrong if everyone loves you.[5]

What about you? What's your general posture toward others and toward yourself?

"YOUR FISH WILL DIE"

If you spent a day in my house toward the beginning of 2022, you would have heard at least one of our daughters singing: "We don't talk about Bruno, no, no, no! We don't talk about Bruno!"

Okay, you might hear me humming along as well.

It's a catchy song from the Disney film *Encanto*. It famously hit number 1 on the Top 100 Billboard charts, and I know we are not supposed to talk about Bruno, but it happened. Bruno, this strange uncle in the family, is a truth-teller, and he uncomfortably says things that people don't want to hear. Think of all the prophets in the Bible. It's not a fun job to be hated by almost everyone for bringing a dose of reality.

In the film, Bruno has been pushed out by his own family and comes to feel he doesn't belong anywhere. The irony is that he is saying things that are pretty obvious: "All your hair will disappear" and "Your fish will die." Everyone's fish will die eventually, but facing the truth is a difficult thing for most people.

In a culture where truth is relative—"you do you, I do me" and "this is my truth" attitudes are prevalent—truth-telling has often become rude and "unkind." Truth-tellers have been pushed away, silenced, and labeled as "unloving." And in fairness, sometimes they are. Bruno probably needed to work on his delivery of bad news. But for followers of Jesus, we are deeply aware of how sin blinds us and that self-deception is very much possible, for "the devil is a liar and no truth is in him" (John 8:44). Paul warned Timothy, "For the time will come when people will not put up with sound doctrine. Instead, to suit their own desires, they will gather around them a great number of teachers to say what their itching ears want to hear. They will turn their ears away from the truth"

(2 Timothy 4:3–4 NIV). And ultimately, we will exchange the truth about God for a lie (Romans 1:25).

When individuals and organizations continue to champion and choose viral recognition, click-bait appeal, influence, reach, emotional manipulation, and profit increase over truth, misinformation becomes the norm. Truth becomes harder to find and less appealing. We are being conditioned to chase and enjoy reality shows more than reality itself.

It doesn't help that we already struggle with *confirmation bias*—the tendency to cherry-pick information that confirms what we already believe. We only hear what we want to hear, and we prefer to spend more of our time looking at information that supports our view. This blurs our ability to see facts and evidence objectively, and what we genuinely believe as "truth" is actually compromised. However, what may sound and feel right to us may not be the truth.

This is why we need more truth, not less. But we also desperately need more grace. Both are so important and crucial to our lives that they're commanded in the Bible: "Therefore each of you must put off falsehood and speak truthfully to your neighbor, for we are all members of one body" (Ephesians 4:25 NIV). There is a way to do it well: with God's grace and mercy, being "kind and compassionate to one another, forgiving each other, just as in Christ God forgave you" (v. 32 NIV).

For many of us who are excited about truth-telling, we need patience. "[There is] a time to be silent and a time to speak" (Ecclesiastes 3:7 NIV). This is wisdom. We need to take a long view of the individual's journey with God. This has been helpful in applying grace to my own life as well. I once heard Craig Ferguson, a comedian and television host, share that there are three things you must always ask yourself before you say anything:

- Does this need to be said?
- Does this need to be said by me?
- Does this need to be said by me, now?[6]

This has helped me catch myself in the name of "truth-telling," releasing my own personal frustrations.

And for many of us who are afraid of truth-telling, we need courage. Perhaps we're afraid of being pushed away and isolated like Bruno. Or we're afraid of being considered judgmental and aggressive. But the Bible repeatedly reminds us not to be afraid. In love and grace we must continue to tell truths to each other. True love indeed shapes us to rejoice with the truth (1 Corinthians 13:6).

The Bible is full of examples of people who spoke the truth in love. Mordecai did not simply sit back after hearing Haman's plot against the Jews. He warned and inspired Esther in her calling and purpose. "Do not think that because you are in the king's house you alone of all the Jews will escape. For if you remain silent at this time, relief and deliverance for the Jews will arise from another place, but you and your father's family will perish. And who knows but that you have come to your royal position for such a time as this?" (Esther 4:13–14 NIV).

Nathan told an engaging story of a rich man who took everything from a poor man to incite rage in David, using it as an anecdote to help David see his own sinful nature in what he had done to Uriah's entire family. "You are that man" is not an easy phrase to use in front of a king who has all the resources to silence you (2 Samuel 12:7). But Nathan did. We are now able to read such beautiful psalms of a broken and contrite spirit from David saying, "Create in me a clean heart, O God, and renew a right spirit within me" (Psalm 51:10). Nathan risked his life to confront his king.

Reuben boldly spoke up against his brothers, risking his own safety. Joseph's brothers had plotted to kill him, throw him into one of the cisterns, and say that a wild animal had eaten him (Genesis 37:20). Verses 21–22 say, "When Reuben heard it, he rescued him out of their hands, saying, 'Let us not take his life.' And Reuben said to them, 'Shed no blood; throw him into this pit here in the wilderness, but do not lay a hand on him.'" Reuben saved Joseph's life with courage and wisdom.

Friends, this is the balance we need. To be people who love and care enough to tell truths that do not guarantee a positive outcome. To stand for the best for everyone, even when it's messy and dangerous. Our position, title, comfort, and reputation shouldn't outweigh another's, and we should speak our care from the core of who we are.

When we prioritize belonging and see each other week in and week out, we can notice patterns and blind spots for one another. Yet we need to form our observations so they're received, otherwise we may do damage. God physically made us in such a way that we can't see ourselves fully. We need reflections to see ourselves. We need others to call out our blind spots.

I remember the following conversation clearly with my men's group. They told me, "This is a safe place to be honest, complain, and be yourself, but we've noticed that as you share and process your life, you complain a lot, especially about your work. We care about you, and since this is a pattern, it might be worth exploring with Jesus."

It was painful to hear, but because I felt valued, this accountability brought greater connection and commitment to the group. I had never thought accountability and belonging would go together. But they do.

ARE YOU A TERRORIST?

On my way home from that men's group, I realized why belonging and accountability were so absent in my life.

And I hated the conclusion I came to: *submission.*

I've been resisting what submission means because accountability with God and others requires submission. It's what it means to live the way of Jesus. Paul wrote, "Submit to one another out of reverence for Christ" (Ephesians 5:21 NIV). I wanted belonging without accountability, without submission. I know this can be a troubling word due to its misuse and abuse but when done right, it's a beautiful picture of what real relationships look like. We even see the submission of Jesus with the Father right before His arrest: "Father, if you are willing, remove this cup from me. Nevertheless, not my will, but yours, be done" (Luke 22:42).

Before you skip this section, remember that every place of belonging has its guidelines on how we ought to live and treat one another, including Eden before the fall. In marriage, you sign an agreement and make a vow before God and others that you will be faithful to each other "till death do us apart." It's similar in our family, workplace, school, city, and country. I remember answering this question among many to become a US citizen: *Do you seek to engage in or have you ever engaged in terrorist activities?*

The nature of such a strong question took me by surprise, but I understood why it was being asked: to guard the safety of people in the United States. It's a reminder that the United States cannot and will not tolerate any form of terrorism if one desires to belong here. And yes, even in Christian community there are guidelines for belonging (in particular, see Matthew 17 and Paul's letters in the New Testament), how we ought to live and treat one another.[7]

Nina and I tell our girls all the time that in our family we treat each other with kindness and respect. And when they break those family values, they have to take a break from their current activity. We tell them their behavior is not okay, and, on occasion, as they walk to their room, one of them will yell out, "Daddy, you are the meanest daddy ever! You're so bossy!"

What they don't realize is that accountability protects and strengthens our family relationships. But this is how we sometimes feel about the commandments in the Bible—that God is robbing us of our freedom and joy. We need to remember that God's commandments are good and are there to protect us.

Dr. C. Stephen Evans, Baylor University philosopher, challenges us to see accountability as a virtue. Instead of seeing accountability primarily as punishment for bad behavior, embracing to live accountably—intentionally becoming a person of honesty, humility, and integrity—can lead to personal growth, stronger relationships, and resilient communities. An excellence that contributes to human flourishing.[8]

This was the case for the ancient Hebrews. Evans talks about how this repeated phrase—*the fear of the Lord*—in the Old Testament was regarded by the ancient Hebrews as a central virtue: a reverent respect in which one acknowledges and embraces the reality that one is accountable to God for one's whole life. The fear of the Lord is the beginning of wisdom because embracing God's heart as our center is the ultimate human good. This is why the ancient Hebrews were able to see and celebrate God's laws as good gifts intended for our flourishing instead thinking He is limiting our freedom and joy (Psalm 119).[9]

We all have our own versions of what the good life is. We redefine sin, morality, and truth to fit our needs, and we do our best to dodge being held accountable and avoid any form of consequences for our actions. We often run away from accountability and mutual submission ultimately because it hurts our pride. But it leads to greater breakdown of self and society, and we live a life never fully belonging anywhere and wonder why we feel so empty and lonely. But what if we began to reframe accountability as a virtue worth embracing?

Accountability invites others to ask hard questions we do not want to hear and opens us up for feedback. That's hard. But when someone cares about us enough to have difficult and awkward conversations in truth and love, and they come alongside us to offer support when we are struggling or not at our best, and when we are able to receive that kind of love, we experience the most beautiful and sacred place of belonging.

Here is the final belonging icon: accountability.

This icon reminds us of Samwise's famous line: "I can't carry it for you, but I can carry you." Whatever image we have when we hear the word *accountability*, I believe that the Bible offers the best picture. Paul said, "Therefore encourage [*parakaleo*] one another and build one another up, just as you are doing" (1 Thessalonians 5:11). The Greek word *parakaleo* literally means to "call alongside." At the end of the day, it's about offering *relational presence*. Ask yourself this: *What does it mean for me to come alongside this person in this very particular moment?*

Furthermore, *parakaleo* is used throughout the New Testament and can mean all these things: comfort, exhort, encourage, and admonish. It's a holistic approach to accountability—to discern and offer exactly what someone needs and not from afar but from their side. We offer our love and presence, and in a world where we tear one another apart, the goal is to build up one another.

This kind of healthy accountability is being able to balance comfort and challenge, safety and growth.

We can find great comfort in knowing that we are not alone in this work! Jesus promises that "he [God] will give you another advocate [*parakletos*] to help you and be with you forever—the Spirit of truth" (John 14:16–17). The Spirit is already at work in advocating, comforting, and revealing truth, and we are invited to join this ministry of the Spirit.

BEST ACCOUNTABILITY PRACTICES: SEVEN INVITATIONS

1. Know the fear.

What is the most difficult thing for them (and you) in accountability? Is it shame? Judgment? The pain of being wrong? Fear of failure or rejection? Naming this will help everyone become less defensive and more compassionate.

2. Give and get permission.

My friend Andy does this so well. He's a dear friend and co-worker at my church. One day, he asked, "Can I speak into your negative energy around a certain leader?" Due to our friendship and trust, I granted him permission to speak into my life. And it was mutual—he gave me permission to speak into his life as well, with this invitation: "Hey David. I trust you and value your voice. Please call me out if I'm off on anything."

3. Pay attention. Be a good coach. Be patient.

It helps to mentally put on a coaching hat. Every great coach knows how to get the best out of each player because they know the current state of each player through careful observation. Paul said, "And we urge you, brothers, admonish the idle, encourage the fainthearted, help the weak, be patient with them all" (1 Thessalonians 5:14). We have to know where they are to give what they most need. Look how Paul identified different forms of accountability depending on where each person was in their journey.

- The idle: *admonish*
- The fainthearted: *encourage*
- The weak: *help*

If you've ever tried to admonish the fainthearted, you know how ineffective that is. Truth-telling isn't only for admonishing. It's for encouragement as well. It's lifting their hearts by calling out beautiful things that are blurry in their lives. This is why accountability is about helping the other person become the person God created them to be.

Patience is a reminder that change is slow for everyone. Take the long view. Take a deep breath. It's okay. God will finish the work He has started in all of us.

4. Care enough to find the courage to speak up.

Are any conflict avoiders reading this? If so, they know the stomach pains that come with scheduling a meeting to have an awkward conversation, messing up, and experiencing relational tension. So we'd rather settle for water cooler conversations and gossip prayer requests. I have found naming our fears to be helpful. "Hey, I care about you and this relationship so this is really hard for me. But I'm sharing this because I'm for you." The use of "I" statements is helpful. "Hey, I felt misunderstood and disrespected when you said ____ at that meeting."

If we do this well, our feedback will be from a place of an invitation for growth instead of from shame and condemnation.

5. Speak specific encouragements and specific prayers.

The word *specific* means "clearly defined." Notice the differences between general and specific here.

GENERAL PRAYER: *I'm praying for you.*

SPECIFIC PRAYER: *I'm asking God that you would have the energy and strength to love and take care of ____ this weekend.*

GENERAL ENCOURAGEMENT: *You are so awesome!*

SPECIFIC ENCOURAGEMENT: *I love how you bring such joy into our conversations and it lifts me up from my negative thought cycle.*

This kind of detailed support shouts out what we ourselves most long for: someone who deeply knows us for who we are and cares enough to speak what they see in us.

6. Find your "log" first.

Matthew 7:5 reminds us to "first take the log out of your own eye, and then you will see clearly to take the speck out of your brother's eye." It's as simple as saying, "Hey, this is something I'm also struggling with" or "Please call me out if you see this in me as well."

This is a difficult area for me to submit to as well. There is a world of difference between leading with *hypocrisy* versus *humility*.

7. Ask better questions.

The best questions create a safe space where we are not making assumptions but are asking the Spirit (the Spirit of truth) to show us what needs to be highlighted. Instead of saying, "You should do this or that," ask,

- What do you sense that God is inviting you to pay attention to?
- How can I support you this week?
- What would be a helpful way for me to encourage your commitment?
- What are the common pitfalls in your life we can rally around for support?

These questions give responsibility and ownership to the individuals. Most of the time, we should accept their answer, even if it's not what we hoped to hear. Pushiness is not accountability. And accountability is not "sin management." It's aligning and joining with what God is already doing in another person's life. In other words, it's helping them recognize God's movements and promptings in their lives. And sometimes, they won't need the help so much as to know you care. This is why accountability without empathy and compassion is what I see as abuse. Now we know why Jesus often led with questions: "Do you want to get well?" to the paralytic was Jesus' way of asking whether he was ready to move from where he was (John 5:6 NIV).

There is a card game I enjoy playing called *We're Not Really*

Strangers. According to their site, it's "a purpose driven card game and movement all about empowering meaningful connections." And I couldn't agree more. The invitation is to come curious and leave connected. It's an incredible tool and safe bridge to get the conversations going with people you want to build deeper relationships with.

Questions include:

- What about me intrigues you the most?
- What lesson took you the longest to unlearn?
- How are you doing, really?

After years of Thai lunch with the group of guys, I was comfortable enough to play this game and ask deeper questions. We were on a drive back from the city and I happened to draw a blank card indicating I could make up a question. So I asked: *What's one area of strength and one of weakness we can grow in?*

We felt safe in this minivan (not just physically!) to speak truths, encourage, and pray for one another. When it was my turn, I remember my buddy Jay saying, "David, you don't need to prove yourself."

He was reminding me that I'm already in and loved both at work and with this group. And I felt he was also challenging me to trust in that reality and give myself away to serve others with all that I am.

I realized at that moment this was what I was looking for all along. And now I have found it. *Belonging.* I didn't want to make the same mistake I made with Paul when I came to America. And I'm so glad I was given permission to open up and I had the safety to accept it.

Accountability Reflection

- Name your fears about accountability. What feels most difficult in being held accountable by someone else?
- As you think about grace and truth, do you have a tendency to emphasize one over the other? If so, why?
- Where is an area of your life that you are not letting anyone hold you to the way of Jesus? In light of this chapter, what might God be highlighting for you to do next?
- Is there anyone with whom you sense God's invitation to lean into truth-telling or encouragement right now? If so, how would you go about that?

Part Three

HOW BELONGING DEEPENS OUR DISCIPLESHIP TO JESUS

'm glad that you've made it this far.
Now, you may be asking:

- How does belonging offer holistic growth in our discipleship and formation to Christlikeness?
- What do we do about the seemingly isolated wilderness journey that Christians face many times in our lives?
- How do we practically cultivate belonging and authentic community in our lives and in our church?

- How do I discern between when to stay or move on from my community?

And maybe the most important question of all:

- What is God highlighting and inviting me to consider in this season of life?

Chapter 8

Being Fully Known and Truly Loved

H ow do these Five Practices work together and guide us to be both fully known and truly loved?

I know it can seem that such perfect belonging and love could only be found in God. Tim Keller has famously said, "To be loved but not known is comforting but superficial. To be known and not loved is our greatest fear. But to be fully known and truly loved is, well, a lot like being loved by God."[1] Absolutely. And, yet, I believe it's possible for Christ followers to imitate this belonging and love. Actually, we are called and empowered to do so by Jesus Himself. He said to His disciples and to all of us: "A new commandment I give to you, that you love one another: just as I have loved you, you also are to love one another" (John 13:34).

As Christians, this imperative is the well we drink from daily: Jesus' constant, reliable, and everlasting love. And from His love and with His power, when we are growing in the Five Practices, we are able to courageously open up all our hidden, broken, and

159

fragmented parts and receive love and belonging from one another. Learning to balance each with the right amount of grace and truth is how belonging and wholeness are both achieved and received.

HOW DO THE FIVE PRACTICES LEAD TO WHOLENESS?

We all long to be fully known and fully loved. That sounds good on paper, yet few of us were taught how that actually works. In his book *Messages*, Matthew McKay talks about the four "selves."[2] As I read it, I realized it would be a helpful paradigm for our conversation on belonging—particularly what it means to be fully seen and known.

According to McKay, the four selves are:

1. The Open Self
2. The Hidden Self
3. The Unknown Self
4. The Blind Self

I believe that only in the context of intentional belonging can we share our *Open Self,* feel safe enough to share and confess our *Hidden Self,* and dream, pray, and celebrate together what the future holds in the *Unknown Self.* And this is how we will come to invite even more safe people to speak to our *Blind Self.* Let's unpack each of these.

The Open Self is the self that's known to oneself and to others. This is the self we feel comfortable talking about. For me, this includes my passion for Korean barbecue, my strong attachment to work and accomplishments, and, of course, my love for Jesus and my beautiful family.

The Hidden Self is known to oneself but unknown to others. Secrets, addictions, painful stories that cause shame—we keep hidden out of fear of rejection. There are many parts we'd rather not talk about.

The Unknown Self is unknown to oneself and unknown to others. It is a lifelong journey to explore our unknown inner terrain with others. Finding new gifts, passions, callings, suppressed memories, and shadows will surprise us in both beautiful and painful ways. We all need someone to walk with us in our celebration and grief along the way.

The Blind Self is unknown to oneself, but known to others. The parts that everyone sees except ourselves are blind spots, and we need mirrors in our lives to point out what we cannot see. Lacking self-awareness (and self-reflection) can be tough to accept, but seeing a personal tendency and moving it to the Open Self can be life-giving.

I think this is a helpful model to have in our journey of deeper belonging. God already knows all these things about us. He knows how distracted and fragmented our thoughts, desires, and wills can be. That's why the greatest commandment encourages us to "love the Lord your God with *all* your heart and with *all* your soul and with *all* your mind and with *all* your strength (Mark 12:30 NIV, emphasis added). That's our whole being—emotional, spiritual, mental, and physical. This invitation is the vision of what it means to be fully human, to be all that God created us to be. To state the obvious, anything less than all is less.

One of life's great temptations and the Enemy's primary work is for us to be unaware of our fragmentation with no real need to turn our entire being toward wholeness. How can we truly begin to live into wholeness until we've discovered and recovered our true selves?

The Five Practices apply to all four parts of self. My prayer is that you would *prioritize* those whom the Spirit may be revealing, then find those with whom you might share *chemistry*, with whom you can be *vulnerable* and *empathize*, with whom you can give and receive *accountability*. Consider how each of the Five Practices might help you uncover more and more of yourself and others.

Let me share a personal example of how this might look in a small way.

MY HIDDEN SELF

I remember when my wife and I welcomed our second baby girl and were struggling financially. We felt overwhelmed and didn't know what to do.

I didn't want to ask anyone for help. I had too much shame. And pride. Now that I was a father of two girls, I did not want anyone to think I couldn't provide and take care of my family. This hidden self of "financial need" wanted to hide in shame but at the same time, it desired to be seen for help.

My wife and I wrestled for a long time with the decision to call my parents. After we made the decision, I couldn't sleep well for a few days leading up to this call. I'd never asked anyone for money since becoming an adult, so I didn't know what to expect. I had so many unanswered questions running around in my head.

What would they think of me?
What if they say no?
What if they say yes?

I eventually mustered up all my strength to call my parents. We caught up for a few minutes but I could sense shame and fear beginning to overwhelm my vocal cords, yes—vulnerability.

I didn't even know how to start the conversation. (I also knew they didn't have much and that didn't help ease my anxiety.)

They knew I was stuttering and rambling on about nothing.

Dad noticed and asked, "Hey, David, what's up?"

"Ummm . . . Dad, we are really struggling and wanted to ask if we could borrow some money."

"How much?" Dad quickly responded.

"About two months of our rent," and I quickly said, "We will pay you back as soon as we can."

Then I lost it. I started to cry with all kinds of tears.

To my parents, tears of shame; to my wife, tears of failure; to my kids, tears of apology; and to myself, tears of frustration.

I said to myself, *I'm just a weak father who is unable to provide for my own family. I didn't even want to hear my dad's response.* So I said, "Dad, I'm so sorry for asking."

"David. We will wire you the money right away."

Then he said these words: "Son, we are here for you at any time you need us. And don't pay us back, because we are family. What we have is yours. I know you have your own family now but you are still our son and we love you. Hang in there."

I didn't know at the time why I felt so deeply seen and loved. I opened my hidden self, waiting for greater shame and rejection from my parents, but it was met with kindness and understanding. Empathy. I thought we needed the money. We certainly did. But I received what I really needed all along. Unashamed love.

The psalmist knew how hearts can be split and distracted in

our own devotion. The well-known prayer "give me an undivided heart" (Psalm 86:11 NIV) is our request. One of my favorite spiritual formation authors, M. Robert Mulholland, summed up this longing beautifully: "Human hearts are hungering for deeper realities in which their fragmented lives can find some measure of wholeness and integrity."[3]

Friends, this kind of belonging offers us the deepest longings of the human soul, which seeks:

Embracing instead of neglect.

Safety in place of fear.

Care instead of abuse.

And spiritual growth in place of stagnation.

. . . where all our divided selves are fully known and deeply loved.

And this isn't some self-fulfillment project. John wrote, "If we love one another, God *lives* in us and his love is made *complete* in us" (1 John 4:12, emphasis added). What this verse is saying is profound—it's not that God doesn't live in us or somehow His love is imperfect—as we love one another, we experience the fullness of God's presence and love. If this is what you really want, you can find it as you engage with and live out the Five Practices. Start to pray about where and how to show them.

In the words of Dallas Willard, "Spiritual formation cannot, in the nature of the case, be a 'private' thing, because it is a matter of whole-life transformation. You need to seek out others in your community who are pursuing the renovation of the heart . . . We must pray that God will lead us to others who can walk with us with Christ—whoever and wherever they may be. And then in patience, stay with them."[4]

Chapter 9

The Gift of Isolation

What if you have tried the earlier tips and now know the Five Practices of belonging but still struggle with feeling lonely? Maybe you are going through a tough season in life and are wondering what to do next as you wait for connection, closeness, and bonding in your community. Perhaps you're thinking, *What's going on? Why is it not working?* And why can't God open up the heavens and physically hand us an exact map for our lives with detailed instructions like Ikea's?

Remember my story of our family's car accident? Let me share what happened during our recovery. I was the one most affected. I suffered a traumatic brain injury—blurry vision and a number of other lingering effects that lasted almost nine months—so I had to step down from my pastoral work to recover. There wasn't an immediate cure; recovery required patience and rest for my body to heal on its own. That was a huge frustration for me. I had recently joined a new church community as a campus pastor—the key task was being available for everything involved in building relationships. What's more, it was the primary place I was finding belonging and purpose. And just like that, everything stopped.

I spent most of my time at home with my family, struggling through my slow adjustment and recovery. I felt grateful for the church community that rallied around us during this difficult season, and we experienced God's love and care through them. Yet I remained largely alone, trying to navigate this new reality while feeling guilty, ashamed, and cut off. Some of it was my own doing: I didn't want to burden others or look needy. And some of it was the unique, personal nature of struggling through any physical or mental-health-related pain.

Life is filled with uninvited detours. When we experience more loneliness even after learning everything in the Five Practices of belonging, we know that it's not a matter of knowing things; life happens and we get thrown off course and wind up alone through no fault of our own. You've experienced the death of a loved one. Your closest friends let you down. You are taken advantage of by the very community leaders that are supposed to shepherd and protect you. Maybe you are currently single, longing for a spouse and wondering why it's not happening. Or you are married but still experiencing distance in the marriage. Your family is shattered. Your spouse or parents left you. You've become an empty nester or a lonely senior. You moved to a new city or became a first-time parent and are entering a new season. Ecclesiastes 3 reminds us that life is designed by God with many seasons, and all of us will, whether we like it or not, encounter these seasons of isolation.

But the point is *how we respond*. How can we respond better next time because of what we learned about what we need as human beings and what it means to be intentional about finding belonging?

RECOGNIZING ISOLATION

In your journey of belonging, you will occasionally find yourself back in isolation. What do you do then?

Recognize every new circumstance brings some necessary adjustment, and it's important to notice and discern between two types of isolation: "self-inflicted" and "God-invited." Biblically, there are ample examples of both. Take the difference between the prodigal son rejecting the father's love in Luke 15 and living painfully alone in the pigs' pen, versus Jesus being led by the Spirit into the wilderness to face the devil alone in Matthew 4. In fact, the devil's familiar question, "Did God *really* say that . . ." pinpoints how discernment makes all the difference.

In *self-inflicted isolation*, people purposefully withdraw from the community, perhaps to find substitute connections to help cope with the pain of life. Perhaps we are following the lies of the Enemy. We do this because we find it easier than reaching out to someone for help. We intentionally run away from God and others and reject any form of wisdom, and this is harmful to our souls and our well-being. Proverbs 18:1 puts it like this: "Whoever isolates himself seeks his own desire; he breaks out against all sound judgment."

For those who are leaders, the most common form of self-inflicted isolation comes by carrying too much of the burden alone. In Scripture, Moses was tasked to lead the Israelites, and as the group became bigger, Moses had to deal with rising complaints and problems in the wilderness. Moses complained that this was all God's fault: "And why have I not found favor in your sight, that you lay the burden of all this people on me?" (Numbers 11:11).

But then he confessed, "I am not able to carry all this people alone; the burden is too heavy for me. If you will treat me like this, kill me at once" (vv. 14–15).

Notice how God didn't respond to Moses' complaints by saying, "Well, good luck Moses. That's the burden of leadership. It's a lonely road and it will cost your mental, physical, and emotional health. Toughen up!"

No. God immediately responded,

> Gather for me seventy men of the elders of Israel, whom you know to be the elders of the people and officers over them, and bring them to the tent of meeting, and let them take their stand there with you. And I will come down and talk with you there. And I will take some of the Spirit that is on you and put it on them, and they shall bear the burden of the people with you, so that you may not bear it yourself alone. (vv. 16–17)

The model God proposed is to gather around ourselves capable leaders to share the burdens together. When we try to be lone heroes we are crushed by the weight of what wasn't supposed to be all ours to begin with.

Therefore, self-inflicted isolation results in *disconnection*, *delusion*, and *dissatisfaction*. If you know your current isolation is self-inflicted, now is the time to lean into the Five Practices!

In *God-invited isolation*, we have a wonderful opportunity to go deeper in our lives with God if we can open ourselves to Him. In these seasons, we face the temptation of becoming frustrated and discouraged. It can seem like no one else understands—even the folks with whom we find meaningful belonging. And if we are not careful to surround ourselves in prayer and awareness of God during these times, we may begin to believe the lies of the Enemy that everyone has deserted us.

And the Enemy will constantly whisper these lies:

You are all alone. No one else feels this way.
No one cares about you. How could they?
God has abandoned you. You were just imagining things before.

This is not a time to give up but to recognize that there are certain seasons and paths that you are meant to go into alone. Sometimes, that means extended solitude. But other times, you are physically near people in your community but are feeling alone (think of Jesus right before His death when His three closest disciples fell asleep). Many followers of Jesus have been confused in recognizing God-invited isolation. It has led some to even leave Jesus altogether.

Remember when Joseph was sold into slavery by his own brothers, then imprisoned in Egypt under false accusations? What injustice! Or when the very people that Moses and Aaron rescued from slavery in Egypt complained and blamed them for the misery in the wilderness? Moses went to the mountaintop alone. Joseph went to prison alone. Hagar was alone in the wilderness after being mistreated by Sarai and Abram. David spent years in a cave running from King Saul after being a loyal and faithful subject. The Bible is filled with stories where God used such unjust seasons to do some incredible inner work on His followers.

Let me not downplay the pain here. We're not talking about a fun and exciting time of growth. It can get as dark and overwhelming as you can imagine. You will feel unseen and overlooked. There is nothing life-giving about injustice. Throughout history, many innocent lives have been scattered and displaced by war, poverty, and evil. And honestly, you might be very much in such a season right now, and those Five Practices seem like they're not that helpful.

But in the stories in the Bible and in our lives, God uses this time for some great purposes.

THREE LESSONS FROM
GOD-INVITED ISOLATION

I've seen God-invited isolation bring about deep change in three particular ways: *examination*, *communication*, and *preparation*.[1] I want to share what I learned about each and what it felt like during my recovery.

Examination

God is always inviting us to examine our lives. But think how rarely we actually do. If you're in one of these God-initiated seasons now, it's a time to pause, rest, and reflect on where you are. It's time to ask tough questions, including your motives. "Do I truly love Jesus with all that I am?" "Am I becoming more like Him?" "Is there an area I may need to pay attention to for my own growth?" "How am I doing with that, honestly?" "Can I fully depend on God?" There is work we can *only* do with God alone, away from all the noise and distractions. Accepting this also tests and exposes the true level of our faith. This is not an easy thing to admit, and for me, it brought some real disappointment: I wanted to be further along than I was in my trust and abilities as a follower. I knew faithful followers of Jesus have found silence, solitude, journaling, spiritual direction, and therapy to be helpful, so I tried to humbly accept the insight and hang on through the struggle.

But I had so many more questions than answers: *What am I looking for? What do I really want? Who am I, really? How is my walk with God?* I sat with my spiritual director to examine with God my deepest fears, doubts, and longings. It hadn't entered my mind I might have anxiety, but soon it emerged—it had been covered over by busyness. Thanks to the guidance and hard work that shifted my focus, this season revealed that my deepest fear was being unimportant, unwanted. And that insight alone led to so much healing.

Communication

There is always a message that God longs to communicate to us. It's desperately needed, but life often gets in the way. We can hear God more clearly when circumstances suddenly change and He finally gets our full attention. In His infinite love for us, it could be what we most need: words of correction, encouragement, or direction. He knows. We simply have to humble and open ourselves to what God might be saying to us, but of course, that's hardly ever so simple. Jesus gave us a word picture of sheep with their shepherd when He said, "My sheep hear my voice, and I know them, and they follow me" (John 10:27). Ultimately, the Good Shepherd's voice is an invitation to grow in intimacy with Him. I'm encouraged to know that faithful followers of Jesus have found *Lectio Divina* (slow and contemplative reading of the Scriptures), prayer, and professional spiritual direction to be helpful.

One more reminder: when you feel a need for an outside perspective, don't think God would prefer you come up with the "answer" all by yourself. God also works through the cords of two, three, or more strands. Reaching out for prayer and communal discernment is absolutely a wonderful way to listen and discern God's voice.

In my long period of waiting to recover, it was clear to me that He wanted me to rest and learn to take care of my body and health, specifically. I'd been running hard, grinding to somehow make a mark in this world, which even for well-meaning Christians is pretty common. He asked me if I could trust Him fully. That was a wake-up call. He gently rebuked me for seeing my family and home life as a task on a checklist instead of God's precious gift for me to love, protect, and care for.

I was doing the same with my own health as well, treating it as a necessary distraction from what mattered at work. He taught me to be content coming to church to receive and learn, instead of using my default posture to teach. My dream was to be a church planter one day, but God invited me to honestly ask whether that was from Him or not. In prayer, discernment, and conversations with trusted people, God began to show me that my next step in ministry was in discipleship and spiritual formation.

Followers of Jesus need the reminder of our true belonging. This season offers that gift: we first and foremost belong to Jesus. Paul said, "You are not your own, for you were bought with a price" (1 Corinthians 6:19–20). This means both things are true: God will never leave or forsake us and God deserves our total allegiance.

Preparation

If we are to follow the way of Jesus, we ought to remember that for much of His life, He was unseen and dismissed. There will also be seasons where you are just as unseen. It's often for the purpose of character development. Think of Jesus before His public ministry—all the years of doing mundane work at home and learning from older leaders. The Bible says, "Jesus grew in wisdom and stature" (Luke 2:52 NIV). Think of Jesus in the wilderness. His faithfulness in the midst of temptations by the Enemy prepared Him for the work ahead. This is not the time to go public and post insights on your social media platforms. Ask for prayer instead. It's an invitation to *hiddenness*, even while the Enemy screams "Prove yourself!"

Henri Nouwen shared that when our lives are hidden, our desire for human affirmations for sustenance are met with the reality that, ultimately, God Himself will give us what we most need. He wrote, "But as we become visible and popular, we quickly grow dependent on people and their responses and easily lose touch with God, the true source of our being. Hiddenness is the place of purification. In hiddenness we find our true selves."[2]

Such solitude with God has a way of naturally preparing us to face bigger things. But our tendency is to want to escape the waiting period. It can feel interminable and test even the strongest of Christians. But if you quit or force the process to go faster (which I have tried to do, many times), it won't work. It's like being stuck in traffic and choosing to drive in the open carpool lane all by yourself. It may feel great at first, but you won't have learned the deeper lessons of patience, contentment despite circumstances, and trust in God's timing. And you will get caught and the consequences could be significant.

It can feel unfair that there isn't any way to speed up character formation. But if you had greater character, would you really want to? Instead, try to relax into it and consider whether there might be an area God is highlighting for growth for the next step of the journey. I know faithful followers of Jesus have found receiving wisdom from mature believers, coaching, and apprenticeship to be helpful in such times.

Another thing you can do is try to ask better questions and be curious about how others have managed their times of preparation. God taught me to listen more attentively to Him and others during my time of waiting to return to pastoring. It wasn't clear what I needed to learn, but while I waited, He grew my heart to love and be loved. It's eye-opening to see that the first characteristic Paul mentioned about love in his famous 1 Corinthians 13 list is *patience*. I've since learned to slow down and work to stay still (just a little bit!).

Seeking wisdom to understand the purpose behind God-invited isolation frees us from pride, resistance, and blaming God, ourselves, or even others in this season. It frees us from believing the lies of the Enemy and anchors us to traverse the rocky terrain of a complicated life with greater perseverance and deeper hope.

This subtle nuance is crucial for transformation:

Self-inflicted isolation offers disconnection, delusion, and dissatisfaction.

God-invited isolation offers distance, discernment, and dependence.

Distance from the chaos of life for rest and reorientation of
    our hearts.
Discernment of our own wisdom versus God's wisdom.
Dependence on God for all things, the giver of life and
    true joy.

WHO LOVES TRAVELING?

Speaking of traversing terrain, let's consider a helpful metaphor. What do you do when there hasn't been an apparent significant change in your life but you still feel isolated or misplaced? What if you are leaning into the Five Practices and you still feel an awkwardness with people or feel out of place? Telling yourself God is preparing you can help the waiting feel more purposeful, but waiting for *what* exactly? And what are you supposed to *do*?

One of my favorite hobbies is traveling. I love exploring new places, eating unique regional foods, and observing how other people live. If I wasn't a pastor, I would certainly want to be a traveling food blogger. But even for those who love traveling, there comes a moment in our journey when we miss our home. We might be in another city or country and will feel misplaced not because anything is bad, but because it's not familiar like home, not where we belong. We are temporarily passing through. That feeling is also true of living on this side of eternity as we wait for Jesus' return. The author of Hebrews reflected on the heroes of our faith:

> These all died in faith, not having received the things promised, but having seen them and greeted them from afar, and having acknowledged that they were strangers and exiles on the earth. For people who speak thus make it clear that they are seeking a homeland. If they had been thinking of that land from which they had gone out, they would have had opportunity to return. But as it is, they desire a better country, that is, a heavenly one. Therefore God is not ashamed to be called their God, for he has prepared for them a city. (Hebrews 11:13–16)

I believe there is great comfort in acknowledging that we are strangers and exiles, traveling and journeying through this earth— that this isn't all there is. These heroes of our faith knew that our home isn't where we were born and raised but a place God has prepared for us (John 14:2–4). And in the book of Revelation, we are told of this future place in more detail:

> Then I saw "a new heaven and a new earth," for the first heaven and the first earth had passed away, and there was no longer any sea. I saw the Holy City, the new Jerusalem, coming down out of heaven from God, prepared as a bride beautifully dressed for her husband. And I heard a loud voice from the throne saying, "Look! God's dwelling place is now among the people, and he will dwell with them. They will be his people, and God himself will be with them and be their God. 'He will wipe every tear from their eyes. There will be no more death' or mourning or crying or pain, for the old order of things has passed away." (Revelation 21:1–4 NIV)

However you feel misplaced, misunderstood, or in a situation where there seems to be no hope, Jesus reminded us that there is much more to our story. And I'm not simply trying to "Christianize" and skip over your pain. My friend Shelene has said to me in tears in the midst of the loss of loved ones and an intense season of racial tension, "David, I'm tired. We're tired. When will this stop? When will all of me belong?" But I see her still getting up each day trusting that God is at work. And He is. Even when it doesn't seem like it.

Jesus knows what it's like to be a stranger and an exile on earth: "Foxes have dens and birds have nests, but the Son of Man has no place to lay his head" (Luke 9:58 NIV). And no matter what your story is, our great source of joy and hope is that we will be united with God Himself. Somehow all the unbelievable wrongs will be made right. We won't be alone, and we will be with the family of God for eternity.

Recently, our family went on a hike with our kids. We thought it was going to be a short hike but apparently I misread the map and by the time we realized it, we were already about halfway deep into it. Our two girls (now ages six and four) hate walking, so we already knew this was going to be a long day. But every time we wanted to give up and turn back, we would see another group coming down, encouraging us that we were almost there and that the view would be worth it. Every time our kids complained (and yes, I did too) and we thought it would be impossible, we'd see another family with small kids trekking along, smiles on their faces. As we passed the other parents, I sensed their camaraderie, encouragement, even a togetherness, like they were with us and proud to be.

As we journey toward Jesus, we will feel tension with the world as we navigate sexuality, politics, ethics, justice, and much more. I'm bolstered by the fact that the word *church* (*ecclesia* in Greek) means "called out ones." This means we should expect we will be ridiculed for journeying on a road that looks foolish. Pastor and author Jon Tyson reminds us that our call is neither silence nor accommodation, but in the culture of compromise, to live with conviction in what he calls *beautiful resistance*.[3] I love that. We will want to take a break, give up, and turn back on our journey, especially when it seems so long and we don't see the point. But we put our hope in Jesus, and we turn toward fellow travelers for encouragement and strength. There is nothing more refreshing than meeting a fellow traveler on that same road.

MY BEST TRAVELING TIPS

I hope if you're in an extended season of loneliness, you feel encouraged to know you aren't alone. Or if you're recognizing this may be such a season, you will know it's purposeful and can be one of the most rewarding times of your life. You don't have to believe that now, but be open to it. We can learn a lot from past travelers who left us with their wisdom in navigating this complex world as we wait for our Lord and Savior Jesus. And if you are in a God-invited isolation, here are some "traveling tips" to take with you that have been passed down to me.

Jesus' Solitude

"Very early in the morning, while it was still dark, Jesus got up, left the house and went off to a solitary place, where he prayed" (Mark 1:35 NIV).

We see Jesus going alone to a solitary place frequently and it was significant enough for the gospel writers to capture this. Solitude is an intentional time to be alone with God. It helps us to be anchored to God in the midst of the chaos and temptations of this world. Here is a helpful way to frame it: *Isolation means I am alone. Solitude means I am alone with God.*

And in this very place, we are reminded of Jesus, who is called Immanuel, *God with us.* Be aware of negative thoughts about God in this season (*God has abandoned me, God doesn't care about me, God doesn't see me*). Solitude helps us anchor ourselves to this truth over and over again: God. With. Us.

Also, remember to lean into honest conversations with God. Even Jesus expressed these painful and raw emotions: "My God, my God, why have you forsaken me?" (Matthew 27:46).

What would it look like to find a quiet place for even five minutes of solitude?

Paul's Request for Prayers

The apostle Paul faced many God-invited isolations. You can hear it in his writings.

> At my first defense, no one came to stand by me, but all deserted me. May it not be charged against them! But the Lord stood by me and strengthened me, so that through me the message would be fully proclaimed and all the Gentiles might hear it. (2 Timothy 4:16–17)

We all carry unique stories that no one has lived through. Even if it feels and looks similar, at the end of the day, it's never the same. We need the comfort and encouragement of the Holy Spirit who searches and knows our hearts. When you face disappointments and even betrayal from your most trusted circle of friends, you need the strength and encouragement from God Himself. And this comes through prayers. Paul asked, "I urge you, brothers and sisters, by our Lord Jesus Christ and by the love of the Spirit, to join me in my struggle by praying to God for me" (Romans 15:30 NIV).

Could you think of one praying person to ask for prayer in this particular season?

Joseph's Reframing

"As for you, you meant evil against me, but God meant it for good, to bring it about that many people should be kept alive, as they are today" (Genesis 50:20).

God is not absent. God is at work in your life. Like Joseph,

when you know you're being targeted, be honest about the intent—
"you meant evil against me." He didn't shy away from speaking
that truth, calling evil what it was and grieving that. But also, don't
let that have the final word in your life. God means to redeem all
evil that befalls us.

Whatever you might be facing, how could you frame it as *"God
meant it for good"*?

I'd like to offer a prayer I wrote out during this season, to
encourage you. It has also helped me shift from focusing entirely
on my own waiting and loneliness to serve others in my own way.

> *Jesus, I remember my wife would talk about her journey of
> loneliness as she first became a mom and all her life's rhythms
> changed. As she is coming out of the season of sleepless nights,
> lack of seeing friends, and not being connected much to the
> community, I am mindful of all the new parents in this sea-
> son. I pray for an extra portion of strength, patience, and
> wisdom for them as my wife sought in this exciting, joy-filled,
> yet surprisingly lonely season.*
>
> *Jesus, I thank You for my mom. I pray that as she battles
> against breast cancer that You would bring full healing and
> strength. She's often home alone and it breaks my heart to be
> living far apart and not being able to see her more. Would
> Your tender, loving grace and comfort be with her?*
>
> *I especially lift up the forgotten and marginalized groups
> in our society and in the church. I cannot fully understand
> their pain and isolation in life but I stand with them in
> prayer. They are treated unfairly and inhumanely by people
> and systems made by human hands. This is not an exhaustive
> list, but my friends, my church community, and my neighbors*

who share in this struggle: the widows, the poor, the elderly, the singles, the immigrants, the disabled, the AAPI community, the African American community, and all those who are under oppressive leaders and regimes and are suffering from unwanted wars. We pray for Your grace. Your justice. Your peace.

Missionaries and their families who have for the sake of the gospel left what is familiar to embrace the unknown, we ask for Your provision as they forge new relationships and communities. I have no idea who is reading this prayer but God, You do. You know their story and the challenges they are facing right now. I pray for Your strength, comfort, and peace that transcends all understanding.

Chapter 10

Cultivate Belonging in
Christian Community

If you are a small group leader, elder, pastor, or someone who cares
deeply about the local church, I'm certain you are thinking about
your own community and asking, How does belonging work in
Christian community and how can we strengthen it?

First things first: as a pastor of a local church myself, trying to
create intentional spaces of belonging in this lonely and disconnected
world is of utmost importance. Why? It's more than trying to get
someone to "stay" at our church. We want to create safe spaces of
belonging where one is seen, known, and loved—where genuine and
meaningful connections are formed and this particular space eventually becomes a place.[1] And in this very place, there is opportunity for
deep formation and transformation into the image of Christ.

It can be difficult to keep this perspective, let alone to accept
even legitimate critique about how we're doing. I am a member of
the church and I know we need real solutions, not just criticism. I
am on the inside with you, in the trenches, praying and thinking

about how to best serve the people God has entrusted to us. It's messy and complex, because we are dealing with humans. The truth is that community is where we are both wounded and healed.

My prayer and hope is to stir some helpful conversations as you think through what God might be inviting your community to consider.

10 PRACTICAL STRATEGIES FOR LEADERS

Lists can be both helpful and overwhelming. I've grouped the lists below into three categories for easier understanding and practical use: Spaces (1–4), Leadership (5–6), and Discipleship (7–10).

Spaces
1. UTILIZE ALL FOUR BELONGING SPACES.
Much of the problem many churches have is that they have not thought critically about how belonging works. I found Joseph Myers's four spaces of belonging framework (with the help of sociologist Edward T. Hall) to be particularly helpful:[2]

PUBLIC: 70+ people (Sunday worship services)
SOCIAL: 20–50 people (mid sized groups)
PERSONAL: 5–12 people (small groups)
INTIMATE: 2–4 people (inner circles)

Churches generally spend most of their energy and resources on two spaces people can belong: Sunday/weekend gathering experiences and small groups. Yet new people—and even many long-time attendees—cannot find belonging and meaningful relationships in these two spaces for many reasons. It's daunting to jump from a large public gathering into a stranger's home where five to twelve people already know each other well. For self-starters, it might be easier, but for those who are naturally timid, we need other on-ramps.

The in-between step, "social space," is regularly dismissed as superficial or not "spiritual" enough. Some are afraid of being distracted from small groups. But social space is best for meeting people and forming loose relationships around commonalities. It offers a low-bar, low-commitment, safer context where people can begin to decide whether they want to get to know someone better. Social spaces often bridge public and personal spaces.

It's helpful in social spaces to form groups around similar interests, activities, or life stages: young professionals, parents of toddlers or teenagers, coffee enthusiasts, creatives, hikers, board game or book lovers, sports fans. Each are a way to create connections that can potentially go deeper. Churches, to their own detriment, neglect these natural connection points.

In addition, intimate spaces must not be ignored. Pastoral care, spiritual direction, coaching, counseling, spiritual friendships, and mentorships can offer soul-connecting bonds. It is the least scalable, the most "inefficient" and resource-laden part of the discipleship pathway in the life of the church, yet we all know from experience it is where we are truly seen and known. It's worth it. Jesus knew it and unapologetically dove into intentional connection with the inner three.

I would also make strategic space for what I call *accelerators of belonging*—retreats, mission trips, camps, intensives, and cohorts, which provide unique opportunities for deep and meaningful connection in a short amount of time with often key bonding ingredients of serving, sacrifice, and sharing built into it.

If we are intentional about these four spaces and accelerators of belonging, Christian communities can avoid settling for being *friendly* versus experiencing *friendship*. Brian Edgar, in his book *God Is Friendship*, warns us, "In the present day, the question is whether churches can be places of genuine friendship rather than friendly churches that are primarily institutions. . . . a friendly church is not necessarily a real community of friends."[3]

Questions to consider:

- Which space of belonging (public, social, personal, and intimate) does your community spend most of its energy and resources fostering?
- What would it look like to cultivate a particular space that needs to be developed?
- Do you personally have a healthy balance of relationships in all belonging spaces?

2. RETHINK SMALL GROUPS.

Small groups are such an integral part of church life. It's where the hope for belonging, intimacy, and transformation first becomes reality. However, because of the exponential increase of loneliness, anxiety, and isolation, it's time to examine the current small group model.

While belonging in each space is important for our flourishing, the Five Practices really begin to apply in personal and intimate spaces. Intimate space is the most difficult to find and build, yet it's the most transformative belonging space for our journey with Jesus. To get there, I think the question we must ask is: *What do small groups do best that no other "space" in the church can offer?*

Sunday worship gathering is essential. A church family needs to worship, commune, serve, give, pray, and hear the Scriptures together. In this large public space, we are all reminded that we are part of something much bigger than ourselves: the body of Christ. Bible studies are small group spaces that help us understand the depths of God's heart for us and learn to live the way of Jesus. Serving and giving can also become small group spaces for living out the mission of Jesus. But we also need another safe space to regularly confess sins, be vulnerable, and share our lives and hear each others' stories, pray for one another's specific circumstances, encourage, and hold each other accountable in living the way of Jesus.

Such connection doesn't happen unless people are experiencing real belonging. We need various small groups, but no matter what kind they may be, we must first train leaders and others in the Five Practices: priority, chemistry, vulnerability, empathy, and accountability.

To listen well and empathize.

To create safe cultures where we can bring our whole selves.

To know the prayer needs and call one another to live the way of Jesus.

And to regularly look for the experiences of grace, truth, forgiveness, healing, and exhortation.

We need *safe* places.

And yes, this affects our approach and strategy to small groups. But if we long for safe, intimate, and transformative communities, there is no easy shortcut. For example,

- if confession and vulnerability are important, then groups should not be larger than about eight to ten people.
- if we know that belonging takes time and trust, we should not constantly split groups for the sake of multiplication. There is

a way to multiply without sacrificing your own safe place of belonging and community.

- if half of the people in the group are committed and the other half are not, it is deflating. The inconsistency and lack of intentionality kills momentum. While we understand that life has its ups and downs, some kind of agreement and prioritization is important.
- if we know this is hard work, choosing and developing leaders who model and create a culture of belonging is of utmost importance.

There are many small group models with different emphases (evangelism, multiplication, Bible study, connection) and strategies (open, closed, seasonal, affinity based). I agree that there is no perfect model for navigating through a disconnected world, but the Five Practices can be fused into a unique model for greater health, belonging, and discipleship.

Start by asking, What is the clear goal and purpose of our small group model? What is the uniqueness of this space that is different (and can be leveraged) from all other spaces of the church community life?

Though there is so much more to this process, this will get you started in the right direction.

3. NAVIGATE THE DIGITAL SPACE.

I live in the heart of Silicon Valley where start-ups, technology, and innovation are interwoven into the fabric of the people we disciple. But this is not unique to that area anymore; it is becoming common everywhere. Here is what we know: in our increasingly networked world, people are spending a significant amount of their time in this digital space both in and outside of our Christian community.

We now have the freedom and ability to not be limited by physical space. We can roam around the globe in this cyberspace, interacting with anyone anywhere. While this allows us to learn from one another and serve the greater good through collaboration, if we are not intentional, we can be shaped by this noncommittal, facade-enabling, and hypermobile space.

We recently did a survey for our online streaming community, asking, "What is the main reason for primarily attending online?"[4] The highest answer, close to 50 percent of the responses, was "convenience," followed by "health-related concerns." While there are legitimate reasons for being online, we must also ask these hard questions:

- How does Jesus of Nazareth (place) and His embodied presence (incarnation) shape our living the way of Jesus?
- Why is it that Gen Z struggles with loneliness more than other generations? Could it be related to the digital age, social media, and fewer opportunities for embodied real-life connections?
- How are we being formed (positively or negatively) by roaming in cyberspace? As many are becoming weary of centralized institutions and power (including the local church), how is cyberspace shaping our view and practice of accountability? How is speed, comfort, and convenience of the digital age shaping our interactions with others in the community?
- What are some ways the digital space can serve the common good of our communities?

4. KIMCHI SOUPS AND KOREAN BBQ:
LEARN FROM ETHNIC COMMUNITIES.

It's a daunting task to show up in a foreign land without a guarantee of a job, without knowing the language and community. Finding and forging meaningful belonging is more than a need—it's a matter of life and death for ethnic communities. Immigrants know what it takes to build community. So we learn from the experts.

Most Korean Christian communities first build churches with three spaces in mind: worship center, kids and youth room, and fellowship hall or cafeteria. This fellowship hall is designed for eating and spending time together after any gathering, especially Sundays (no matter the size of your community). It's a massive logistical undertaking for any church to cook for tens to hundreds—sometimes thousands—of people, but like the early church in Acts, "they devoted themselves to the apostles' teaching and the fellowship, to the breaking of bread and the prayers" (Acts 2:42). The cafeteria naturally encourages conversations with those whom you sit next to and provides one less barrier to overcome in building relationships. For newcomers, instead of walking straight to the parking lot after the service, now there is an opportunity for connection. And yes, to smell Korean barbecue (on special holidays but I wish it was every week) while singing songs about Jesus. Where else would we want to be?

I would confidently say, having spent significant time participating and working for Korean American churches, that building community alongside prayer are the great strengths and gifts to learn from the ethnic church.

It's totally okay if space and budget don't allow for this. I pastor in Silicon Valley, so I know the challenges of real estate! There are many creative ways to build these intentional lingering spaces. From lawns to small cafes, finding available spaces and building a need to linger is all it requires to get started. Take an inventory around your church community—see the spaces God has already given you and be creative with how meaningful conversations can be fostered in those places.

Leadership

5. KNOW THAT LEADERS AREN'T IMMUNE.

I've heard from an administrator of a pastor's job posting site that Sunday nights get the highest amount of web traffic. I'm sure it's for various reasons but I wonder if one is that many pastors and church leaders are lonely and do not have their own spaces for belonging. Churches that don't emphasize meaningful belonging result from leaders who don't value their own. I know this firsthand.

- We are tired of pastors and leaders who can't prioritize people and have a hard time caring for others.
- We are tired of pastors and leaders who don't like to listen well and who talk over others constantly.
- We are tired of pastors and leaders who pretend and can't be vulnerable and honest about their own journeys.
- We are tired of pastors and leaders who think stage, fans, and followers on social media are their authentic community, a place of belonging.
- We are tired of pastors and leaders who refuse to regularly confess sin and be accountable to others.

In our loneliness and desperation, we must be careful not to look for belonging and significance in dangerous spaces whether it be inappropriate relationships fostered by emotional entanglement, titles and platforms that feed our need for more power and control, to our attachment to money and its false promises of salvation.

We are looking for pastors and leaders who can offer a safe and meaningful place of belonging where the deep, transformative work of God can take place. This means we need to consider one thing: Do pastors and leaders in your community have a safe place not to "lead" but simply regularly participate in the Five Practices for the sake of their own health? If not, what would it look like to foster that in your context?

6. INVITE OTHERS IN.

The disciples tried to protect their Master—His time and focus. Matthew observed, "Then people brought little children to Jesus for him to place his hands on them and pray for them. But the disciples rebuked them. Jesus said, 'Let the little children come to me, and do not hinder them, for the kingdom of heaven *belongs* to such as these'" (19:13–14 NIV, emphasis added).

I get it. Whether your community is small or large, there is a challenge to meet all the needs of your people. There are many good things that fight for the attention of the senior leadership team, and it's the responsibility of the leaders to be thoughtful and wise with the resources.

At the same time, we should not intentionally hinder groups in our community from meaningful engagement. Jesus said to His leadership team: "Do not hinder children, for they belong here." What would it look like to invite diverse voices to the seat of leadership? Which groups are constantly left out in your decision-making process and why?

Discipleship
7. OFFER HOLISTIC DISCIPLESHIP TO THOSE WHO ARE DIFFICULT, HURTING, AND STUCK.

We can't keep telling people to belong to our community without giving practical support and tools for belonging. Many of our people carry anxiety, distrust, trauma, and emotional and mental health related issues. It affects our social skills, emotional intelligence, and our ability to belong. I understand that most churches won't have all the resources—which means intentional partnerships with counseling centers, therapists, life skills coaches, and mental health experts are needed.

At the same time, experiencing a safe belonging space is crucial for those who are deeply wounded. I remember getting ready to teach my first sermon at my church. I was anxious from my own fears of insecurity and trying to measure up to all the gifted teachers that we have on staff. My pastor Steve said, "David, we hired you so we can hear from you, not me. Be yourself and trust the Spirit of God in you!" This is the kind of belonging culture Steve offered. After the message, even though I knew I had so much work to do to get better, Steve gave me a hug and said a few words of encouragement and support.

We need to ask ourselves, What if in addition to constantly inviting everyone to join an intentional community, we actually offer practical tools that can foster and strengthen skills as we navigate common challenges of relationships and belonging?

8. SERVE TO BELONG.

We all know how crucial serving is in the life of the church and the formational journey of all who follow Jesus. When we can serve the church with the particular gifts God has entrusted to us, our commitment, joy, and a sense of belonging increase. Let me share two thoughts that could be helpful for us. First, serving is often attached to helping execute the needs of the church. As a member of the family, we all play our part. This is both important and good. But we tend to forget that God has also given each individual unique gifts to build up the body of Christ. Churches rarely tap into them. For example, our community constantly runs into problems related to church databases and technology while a significant portion of our people are working in global tech platforms in Silicon Valley! And yet, we are only in the beginning stages of inviting our members to use their God-given gifts and passions to help solve our problems. Helping our people identify their gifts, passions, and wiring, and providing space for innovation and unique serving opportunities per their giftedness can be life-giving and increase ownership, and thereby belonging (there is a reason why belonging can also be defined as possession or ownership).

Second, one big concern that many Christian leaders have about belonging is the "holy huddle." In our search for belonging, we can easily become inward and myopic within our smaller community and even prevent our efforts toward living out Jesus' prayers for the unity of God's family (John 17). This is why serving outside our walls—partnerships and collaborations with other organizations and churches—helps us resist the temptation to turn inward and reminds us that we also belong to the global church and the kingdom of God.

9. PROVIDE CLARITY OF MISSION AND MEMBERSHIP.

Every community has its own unique mission statements and values. Be clear about your mission and calling up front. Don't bait and switch. And don't apologize. Be kind but firm on your boundary lines. This can alleviate many headaches and heartaches in the future. Here is what I mean.

Some may ask, shouldn't the small group spend more time in Bible study than praying, sharing, and confessing sins? How come the worship songs are only twenty minutes on Sunday morning? Bonhoeffer's most famous quote on community in *Life Together* still rings true today: "The person who loves their dream of community will destroy community."[5] They have their own idea of what a community *should* look like and bring their own agendas and expectations instead of learning and listening to what God is already doing there. When there is clarity around why we do certain things, it helps us eliminate unnecessary conflicts.

Belonging requires a formal commitment. Any kind of formal agreement and contract can feel less welcoming, but it actually guards and strengthens belonging. In our noncommittal culture, commitment is an invitation to settle down. Stay. Find home.

Think of your marriage, school, team, or workplace. Each requires an agreement on how we ought to live and work together. That consensus is there to protect and honor one another, not to control and manipulate. Church membership increases belonging for those who are in and inspires others to join this family. It's not a "we are better than you" posture to those who have yet to join. It's identifying and giving clarity around who is in with this mission and agreement to live and act within this space.

Depending on the Christian community, they may emphasize one over the other: "believe in order to belong" or "belong before believing." Healthy Christian communities must be able to champion and hold both tensions well: *belong* (no matter where you are on your journey, you are welcomed and loved here) and *believe* (clarity about what it looks like to be all in with us: saying yes to Jesus and to the mission of this community).

Do you have clarity around your mission and what it means to belong in your community? What would it look like for your community to hold both the invitation to belong and believe?

10. START NOW—IT'S NOT TOO LATE!

If you are a parent reading this book, you might be overwhelmed thinking about your own children and how they might be experiencing belonging at home. As we discussed in chapter 2, family is the very first place where God designed us to receive love, care, and support because we are born into this world into a family. This is the first place where we should experience true belonging by receiving meaningful connection and intimacy. Our kids learn how to love and be loved, to know and be known, and to see and be seen.

For now, I'll get you started with one small and effective step that can immediately create a safe belonging space for your kids. Safe belonging space means being *emotionally available*.

Start by every day carving out ten minutes of uninterrupted, no screens, and no agenda time for your kids. What you are saying by offering this posture is "I'm here for you. I'm available to really hear and see you because you matter." This may not seem like a lot, but for the kids, this kind of attention, care, and support is what they have been waiting for (even if they don't show it). These ten minutes will add up and set up a new culture at home. And when they *really* need you, they will remember that you are safe and will hold them with love and empathy, grace and truth.

As you can see, this chapter alone could be its own book. I've only scratched the surface for each of these points. It requires longer and deeper conversations, prayer, and strategies to foster belonging.

It is a slow but needed work. And again, as a pastor, I totally empathize with managing the whirlwind of the weekend and the ministry of the entire church. But we can all agree we deeply care about helping people who are disconnected and displaced to find their spiritual home, a family where they belong.

I encourage you to take some time examining your entire discipleship pathway (including on-ramps and next steps) to see what God might be highlighting for you to strengthen. Every community has its own stories and journey of belonging. If any one of the invitations in this chapter can be helpful for you and your community, it would be an honor to listen and support what God might be highlighting in this season.

Most importantly, I pray with Paul's prayer for the church in Corinth, reminding us of the triune God—the best model of belonging to one another in community, empowering us with their own unique gifts and presence.

> May the grace of the Lord Jesus Christ, and the love of God, and the fellowship of the Holy Spirit be with you all. (2 Corinthians 13:14 NIV)

Conclusion

DISCERNING TO STAY OR MOVE ON

Have you ever thought about leaving your Christian community?

I just can't take it anymore.
I can't grow here.
I need something different.

There are plenty of great reasons for leaving your community: moving to a new city because of school, job, or family situation; experiencing toxic and abusive leadership; or responding to God's call to serve in a new community. And if you are currently exploring leaving your Christian community, my prayer is that this section serves as a prayerful discernment space of God's invitation, not one of shame and condemnation.

As you pray, seek godly wisdom and counsel, and discern the leading of the Spirit and the motivation of your heart, have you asked yourself, when is the right time to move on from my community?

Joseph H. Hellerman, pastor and professor of New Testament, in his book *When the Church Was a Family*, wrote:

Long-term interpersonal relationships are the crucible of genuine progress in the Christian life. People who stay also grow. People who leave do not grow. We all know people who are consumed with spiritual wanderlust. But we never get to know them very well because they cannot seem to stay put. They move along from church to church, ever searching for a congregation that will better satisfy their felt needs. Like trees repeatedly transplanted from soil to soil, these spiritual nomads fail to put down roots and seldom experience lasting and fruitful growth in their Christian lives.[1]

Is this you? When things get hard, do you move from one place to another? Is this a repeated pattern in your life? Do you have long-term interpersonal relationships or are you still searching for your "perfect" person or church?

Before you answer these questions, I'll be the first to admit that I've done this to many of my close friends throughout my life. I would rather not work through conflict or, if I see that there is something I just don't like in them, I'll quickly move on with my life. At the end of the day, I see selfishness and ego getting in the way of God's deep work through the people He has sent to my life.

I would like to share three observations from years of pastoral ministry.

First, we need more resilient followers of Jesus who won't give up easily. Many tend to believe that moving to a different community is one of the best ways to grow in our spiritual lives, to fix our own frustration and stagnation. Hoping for a fresh start somewhere else would do the trick. It seems like it's always the first option we consider. Could it be that all the stirrings of our hearts are for a renewed and greater commitment to endure and be more all-in? *What if the best way to grow is by staying?*

Second, we need more courageous followers of Jesus who won't fear man. I've seen the power of "Us-ness" prevent individuals from going to the place God is showing them. This is more common in ethnic communities—where in its beautifully communally centered emphasis, we stay much longer than God intended due to our own lack of courage and potential shame from the community. They see leaving as a weakness of faith, selfish, and a betrayal of the community. Could we have individual callings that may differ from the entire group? *What if the best way to grow is by moving?*

Last, there was a question God asked me many years ago in my previous community. I was in a place of deep hurt, frustration, and anger at the way I had been treated by some of the leaders over the years. I had every reason to leave. I was in a meeting with one of those leaders and clearly, my heart was filled with all sorts of evil, including deep animosity and hatred. But by God's grace, I remember God posing this question: David, will you commit to loving this leader well?

"No," I said. "This is not the right time for that question."

But I knew that was the right question.

I spent six more months in that community. Things didn't resolve but with intense inner work, I was able to leave the place and able to love and bless those leaders with sincerity. This doesn't mean you should stay in a toxic culture or be a pushover. This doesn't mean I'm done working through all my trauma. But this does mean one thing. Dallas Willard once said: "The main thing that God gets out of your life . . . is the person you become."[2] Whatever decision you are faced with in your community, our highest commitment as followers of Jesus is to become a person of love.

In *Better Decisions, Fewer Regrets*, the question Andy Stanley asks at the end of a healthy decision-making process is: What does love require of me?[3]

In other words, which decision will better help you become a person of love?

THE CHRISTIAN LIFE ISN'T JUST DIFFICULT TO DO ALONE— IT'S IMPOSSIBLE

I've heard it said many times that how you lived your life is truly shown at your funeral service. And every time I heard one of those motivational speeches, I told myself to live in such a way that, at my funeral, thousands who were impacted by my work and ministry will show up to grieve and celebrate my life. This definitely would be Instagram friendly.

But now, my prayer is that I would have a handful of close friends who know me from inside out, my highs and lows, my shortcomings and quirks. And I hope they say I cared deeply and modeled a strong commitment to their journey and everything that came with it. That I sat with them in their pain. That I celebrated their huge milestones. That we prayed together when temptations came our way. That we confessed our darkest sins. This would be far less Instagramable.

But this is the life I want.

And I've still got a way to go.

So one day at a time.

I say these words out loud as a prayer and declaration, for myself and for all of us. Maybe you can pray this with me:

God, please help me learn these Five Practices:

PRIORITY: to value relationships in a me-centered world
CHEMISTRY: to enjoy one another's presence
VULNERABILITY: to be open, even when it's difficult
EMPATHY: to lean in and care for one another
ACCOUNTABILITY: to carry others even if it costs me, and
    allow others to carry me

And I'm adding this great, simple prayer from Flannery O'Connor: "Lead us toward those we are waiting for, those who are waiting for us."[4]

I recommit to this afresh, even now.

We have this mantra for our church community:

The Christian life is not just difficult to do alone. It's impossible.

We say this regularly because, surrounded by technology and all its offerings, we deceive ourselves into thinking we can do life alone. I thought I could be a hero and be the first Christian in history to make it on my own. After all, I'm a pastor, right?

One thing I found strange as a teen after moving with my family to America was that the kids would eat at the same table as adults. I thought to myself, *They don't belong there.* It was awkward for me to watch kids talk to the adults and be engaged in the same conversation. In Korea, I was used to kids eating at the kids' table. I always knew where I belonged. I knew my place.

When reading the Gospels, I am drawn to Jesus making space and offering belonging to everyone, particularly to those who were deemed undeserving by society. Jesus intentionally broke every barrier and division made by humankind and offered belonging to all: children, women, people with disabilities, sinners and tax collectors, and the poor. Even to Judas, Jesus offered His table of love and grace.

The goal of this belonging journey has been to help you know how to find your place. And yet, as followers of Jesus, when we model what Christ did from a place of belonging, we can offer that same belonging and see it grow with those who have not yet found it.

In the process, don't be surprised if you end up experiencing life-giving belonging from them as well.

Acknowledgments

S o many have impacted my journey of belonging and provided love, grace, truth, and a safe place to be seen, known, and loved.

Let me start with my parents. Thank you for loving me so well and introducing me to my greatest treasure, Jesus. I am fully aware that I would not be where I am today without your prayers. 사랑하고 감사합니다.

Jon, it's an understatement to say we've been through a lot together. I am so proud of watching your beautiful family from afar—Heena, Shiloh, and Konah. My one wish is that we lived closer!

To my men's group, TNI (Tuesday Night, Inc.): Josh, Jeff, Dave, Rev, Ryan, and Matt, I look forward to coming every Tuesday night to process together our lives and consider what God might be inviting us to consider each week. Thanks for holding me when I'm hurting, waking me up to reality when I'm confused, and pointing me to what matters most when I forget. And our group texts—prayer requests, gifs, random ideas, podcast recs, inappropriate comments, accountability. See you on Tuesday!

To my FF: Dave, Josh, Jay, and Andy, thanks for offering a safe and fun space where I can be me, life isn't all about work, and what truly matters is integrity and loving our families well.

WestGate Church family, thank you for loving our family so well. We have found desperately needed healing here. We will never forget how you rallied around us during our family's difficult seasons. Steve and Dana, we are so grateful to you for building such a loving community where many can find refuge and restoration. And to the elders and the executive team, thank you for entrusting me to foster spaces of belonging, to build authentic community, and to help create clear and helpful pathways and next steps for people to learn, connect, and grow in their journey with Jesus.

Shoutout to our Discipleship and Formation team—Nicole, Melissa, Ruth, and Claire—you've made it a joy to come to work every day. And yes, we've had too much coffee, boba, and Thai. To our life group leaders and shepherds, you are the heroes truly embodying this book, creating sacred spaces of belonging where people are known and loved well. And to the entire WestGate staff, I am honored to learn and serve alongside you.

Teri, my spiritual director, thank you for helping me unpack and discern God's movements in my life with such warmth and love. To Jeff, Andy, and Will—love you guys and praying that God would create even more opportunities for our paths to cross!

Jenny, my incredible editor, and the entire Nelson team, thank you for believing in me and my book. And Janene for getting the book to the finish line! Jessie, thanks for making my ideas visually come alive with the Belonging icons! Mick, I could not have met a better writing coach! Sarah, thank you for lending your sharp mind and attention to details for this project. Josh, Jeannie, and Hansub, I looked forward to receiving your feedback—thanks for your wisdom and insight!

Nina, Skylar, and Zoey, my hope is that you experience belonging at home. I pray that God would help me to continue to create safe spaces where you are seen, known, and unconditionally loved. And Nina, finally no more late night questions about BELONGING!!!

Thank you, Jesus, for extending your love and friendship. Grateful to be part of the larger family of God.

Notes

Introduction

1. "Loneliness," *Psychology Today*, accessed July 23, 2021, https://www
.psychologytoday.com/us/basics/loneliness.
2. Liana DesHarnais Bruce et al., "Loneliness in the United States: A 2018
National Panel Survey of Demographic, Structural, Cognitive, and Behavioral
Characteristics," *American Journal of Health Promotion* 33, no. 8 (November 2019):
1123–33, https://journals.sagepub.com/doi/full/10.1177/0890117119856551.
3. "Loneliness and the Workplace," Cigna, January 23, 2020, https://www.multivu
.com/players/English/8670451-cigna-2020-loneliness-index/, quoting *Cigna U. S.
Loneliness Index* (Bloomfield, CT: Cigna, 2018), https://www.cigna.com/static
/www-cigna-com/docs/about-us/newsroom/studies-and-reports/combatting
-loneliness/loneliness-survey-2018-full-report.pdf.
4. "About," David Kim, accessed September 11, 2022, https://
www.davidjanghyunkim.com/about.
5. "Books," David Kim, accessed September 12, 2022, https://
www.davidjanghyunkim.com/books.
6. For those who are interested, I received a BA in Biblical Studies at Gordon
College, and an MDiv and ThM in Theology and Culture from Gordon-Conwell
Theological Seminary.

Chapter 1: The False Connection Cycle

1. Emma Gray, "Opinion: Abercrombie and Fitch's Racist, Sexist,
Fatphobic American Fantasy," MSNBC Opinion Column, April 22, 2022,
https://www.msnbc.com/opinion/msnbc-opinion/new-netflix-documentary
-takes-down-abercrombie-fitch-n1294716.
2. Courtney L. McCluney et al., "The Costs of Code-Switching," *Harvard Business
Review*, November 15, 2019. https://hbr.org/2019/11/the-costs-of-codeswitching.
3. Simon Kemp, "Digital 2021: The Latest Insights into the 'State of Digital,'" We
Are Social, January 27, 2021, https://wearesocial.com/uk/blog/2021/01
/digital-2021-the-latest-insights-into-the-state-of-digital.

4. Fight the New Drug, "How Many People Are on Porn Sites Right Now? (Hint: It's a Lot!)," April 5, 2022, https://fightthenewdrug.org/by-the-numbers-see-how-many-people-are-watching-porn-today/.

5. Christian Zilles, "The Social Media Paradox, Revisited," Social Media HQ, January 6, 2022, https://socialmediahq.com/the-social-media-paradox-revisited/.

6. Mark Granovetter, "The Strength of Weak Ties," *American Journal of Sociology* 78, no. 6 (May 1973): 1360–80, https://www.cse.wustl.edu/~m.neumann/fl2017/cse316/materials/strength_of_weak_ties.pdf.

7. Joshua Freedman, "State of the Heart 2018," Six Seconds, accessed July 25, 2022, https://www.6seconds.org/2018/09/05/state-of-the-heart-2018/.

8. Andy Crouch, *The Tech-Wise Family: Everyday Steps for Putting Technology in Its Proper Place* (Ada, MI: Baker Books, 2017), 20.

9. "#술은내친구," Google, accessed January 2, 2021, https://www.google.com/search?q=%23술은내친구.

10. Phil Longstreet, "Life Satisfaction: A Key to Managing Internet & Social Media Addiction," *Technology in Society* 50 (August 2017): 73–77, https://www.sciencedirect.com/science/article/abs/pii/S0160791X16301634.

11. "Loneliness and the Workplace," Cigna, January 23, 2020, https://www.multivu.com/players/English/8670451-cigna-2020-loneliness-index.

12. This survey was conducted on August 4, 2019.

13. At the 1998 Academy Awards, *Titanic* was nominated for all fourteen categories and won eleven of them.

Chapter 2: Barriers to Belonging

1. I know you're dying to know what school I applied to, but I'm not going to tell you for two reasons: one, I don't want the college I eventually chose to feel bad, and two, it still hurts too much to talk about.

2. Bessel van der Kolk, *The Body Keeps the Score: Brain, Mind, and Body in the Healing of Trauma* (New York: Penguin, 2015), 21.

3. W. David O. Taylor, *Open and Unafraid: The Psalms as a Guide to Life* (Nashville: Nelson Books, 2020), 138–39.

4. Daniel Siegel and Tina Payne Bryson, *The Whole-Brain Child: 12 Revolutionary Strategies to Nurture Your Child's Developing Mind* (New York: Bantam, 2012), xii.

5. "The Power of Touch," Baby Sensory, accessed July 27, 2022, https://www.babysensory.com.au/power_of_touch.

6. Milan and Kay Yerkovich, *How We Love: Discover Your Love Style, Enhance Your Marriage*, expanded ed., (Colorado Springs: WaterBrook, 2017), 296.

7. John Bowlby, *A Secure Base: Parent-Child Attachment and Healthy Human Development* (New York: Basic Books, 1988).

8. If this is something you struggle with, finding a good therapist is a wonderful place to explore the *why* behind the *what*.

9. Teresa of Avila, *The Way of Perfection*, E. Allison Peers, trans. and ed., from the critical edition of Silverio de Santa Teresa (New York: Image Classics, 1991).

10. David Carder et al., *Secrets of Your Family Tree: Healing for Adult Children of Dysfunctional Families* (Chicago: Moody Publishers, 1995), 20.

Chapter 3: Practice #1: Priority

1. Bronnie Ware, *Top Five Regrets of the Dying: A Life Transformed by the Dearly Departing* (Carlsbad, CA: Hay House, 2019), quoted in Susie Steiner, "Top Five Regrets of the Dying," *The Guardian*, February 1, 2012, https://www.theguardian .com/lifeandstyle/2012/feb/01/top-five-regrets-of-the-dying?cat=lifeandstyle&type =article.
2. Kelly-Ann Allen, "Making Sense of Belonging," *InPsych* 41, no. 3 (June 2019), https://psychology.org.au/for-members/publications/inpsych/2019/june /making-sense-of-belonging#:~:text=Belonging%20is%20defined%20as %20a,proximity%20to%2C%20others%20or%20groups.
3. Sebastian Junger, *Tribe: On Homecoming and Belonging* (New York: Twelve, 2016), 18.
4. Christopher K. Chung and Samson J. Cho, "Conceptualization of Jeong and Dynamics of Hwabyung," *Psychiatry Investigation* 3, no. 1 (February 2006): 46–54, https://www.psychiatryinvestigation.org/upload/pdf/0502006005.pdf.
5. John Mark Comer, *The Ruthless Elimination of Hurry: How to Stay Emotionally Healthy and Spiritually Alive in the Chaos of the Modern World* (Colorado Springs: WaterBrook, 2019), 20.
6. Curt Thompson, *The Soul of Shame: Retelling the Stories We Believe About Ourselves* (Downers Grove, IL: IVP, 2015), 138.
7. James K. A. Smith, *You Are What You Love: The Spiritual Power of Habit* (Ada, MI: Brazos, 2016), 2.
8. Though Dunbar's number is cited in his earlier work, I recommend reading his latest research: Robin Dunbar, *Friends: Understanding the Power of Our Most Important Relationships* (Boston: Little, Brown and Company, 2021).
9. Full credit: I first learned this practice from my pastor Steve Clifford. He's been doing this for decades since so many things fight for his attention.
10. C. S. Lewis, *The Four Loves* (1960; repr., New York: HarperOne, 2017), 114.
11. David Brooks, *The Second Mountain: The Quest for a Moral Life* (New York: Random House, 2019), 56.
12. James Clear, *Atomic Habits: Tiny Changes, Remarkable Results: An Easy & Proven Way to Build Good Habits & Break Bad Ones* (New York: Avery, 2018), 24.
13. Henri J. M. Nouwen, *Bread for the Journey: A Daybook of Wisdom and Faith* (New York: HarperOne, 2006), s.v. "January 19."

Chapter 4: Practice #2: Chemistry

1. Steve Bang Lee, "Christian Tribe vs. Tribal Christian. There's a Difference," *Bang Blogs*, October 5, 2021, https://www.bangblogs.org/new-blog/2021/10/4 /christian-tribe-vs-tribal-christian-theres-a-differencenbsp.
2. Rosaria Butterfield, *The Gospel Comes with a House Key: Practicing Radically Ordinary Hospitality in Our Post-Christian World* (Wheaton, IL: Crossway, 2018), 95.
3. Parker Palmer, *A Place Called Community* (Wallingford, PA: Pendle Hill, 2013), Kindle edition.
4. C. S. Lewis, *The Four Loves* (1960; repr., New York: Harcourt, 1988), 81.

5. Alexandra Owens, "Tell Me All I Need to Know About Oxytocin," *Psycom*, September 23, 2021, https://www.psycom.net/oxytocin.

6. Kelly Campbell, Nicole Holderness, and Matt Riggs, "Friendship Chemistry: An Examination of Underlying Factors," *Social Science Journal* 52, no. 2 (June 2015): 239–47, https://www.ncbi.nlm.nih.gov/pmc/articles/PMC4470381/.

7. Lewis, *Four Loves*, 65.

Chapter 5: Practice #3: Vulnerability

1. I highly recommend reading Dr. Curt Thompson's work on shame: *The Soul of Shame: Retelling the Stories We Believe About Ourselves* (Downers Grove, IL: IVP, 2015).

2. Alice Fryling, *Mirror for the Soul: A Christian Guide to the Enneagram* (Downers Grove, IL: IVP, 2017), 25.

3. Carissa Quinn, "Connected: Humanity's Design in the Biblical Story," Bible Project, 2019, https://bibleproject.com/blog/connected-humanity-design/.

4. The Gottman Institute, "3 Ways to Make a Better Bid for Connection," accessed July 30, 2022, https://www.gottman.com/blog/3-ways-to-make-a-better-bid -for-connection/.

5. Lewis, *Four Loves*, 121.

6. Malcolm Gladwell, *Outliers: The Story of Success* (Lebanon, IN: Back Bay, 2011), 177.

7. Rich Villodas, *The Deeply Formed Life: Five Transformative Values to Root Us in the Way of Jesus* (Colorado Springs: WaterBrook, 2021), 134–36.

8. Brené Brown. *Daring Greatly: How the Courage to Be Vulnerable Transforms the Way We Live, Love, Parent, and Lead* (New York: Avery, 2015), 113.

9. Dietrich Bonhoeffer, *Life Together: The Classic Exploration of Faith in Community* (San Francisco, CA: HarperOne, 1978), 119.

10. A. W. Tozer, *Three Spiritual Classics in One Volume: The Knowledge of the Holy, The Pursuit of God, God's Pursuit of Man* (1961; repr., Chicago: Moody Publishers, 2018), 13.

11. Curt Thompson, *The Soul of Desire: Discovering the Neuroscience of Longing, Beauty, and Community* (Downers Grove, IL: IVP, 2021), 63.

12. Steve Clifford, personal communication.

13. Flannery O'Connor, *Mystery and Manners: Occasional Prose* (New York: Farrar, Straus & Giroux, 1970), 35.

14. Andy Gridley, *Three Little Words with Big Power* (lecture, June 26, 2021, WestGate Church, San Jose, CA).

15. Brown, *Daring Greatly*, 159.

Chapter 6: Practice #4: Empathy

1. Brown, *Daring Greatly*, 81.

2. Sara Konrath, "Episode 95: The Decline of Empathy and the Rise of Narcissism," December 4, 2019, in *Speaking of Psychology*, podcast, MP3 audio, 45:31, American Psychological Association, https://www.apa.org/news/podcasts/speaking-of-psychology/empathy-narcissism; Judith Hall and Mark Leary, "The U.S. Has an

Empathy Deficit," *Scientific American*, September 17, 2020, https://www
.scientificamerican.com/article/the-us-has-an-empathy-deficit/.

3. Businessolver, 2021, *Empathy Study Executive Summary*, https://resources
.businessolver.com/c/2021-empathy-exec-summ?x=OE03jO.

4. Chuck DeGroat, *When Narcissism Comes to Church: Healing Your Community from
Emotional and Spiritual Abuse* (Downers Grove, IL: IVP, 2020).

5. In Korean, they would say "nunchi," literally translated as "eye-measure."
Obviously, too much of it can make us hypervigilant and cripple our own
humanity to be ourselves.

6. Speaking of the East, let me introduce you to another Korean word, *jeong*, a
difficult word to translate. It refers to the "deep emotional and psychological bonds
that join Koreans." This can be a beautiful picture of incredible affection, care,
and unity, yet it can demand unrealistic allegiance and unconditional loyalty to a
fault. Christopher K. Chung and Samson J. Cho, "*Conceptualization of Jeong and
Dynamics of Hwabyung*," *Psychiatry Investigation* 3, no. 1 (February 2006): 46–54,
https://www.psychiatryinvestigation.org/upload/pdf/0502006005.pdf.

7. Scot McKnight, "Empathy Is a Virtue," *Jesus Creed* (blog), *Christianity Today*,
March 15, 2021, https://www.christianitytoday.com/scot-mcknight/2021/march
/empathy-is-virtue.html.

8. Steve Cuss (@stevecusswords), Twitter, May 24, 2019, 8:47 a.m., https://twitter
.com/stevecusswords/status/1131919663061823488?lang=en.

9. The Greek word here is *sympatheō*. While it can mean "sympathize" in some
contexts, "empathize" is a more accurate translation of this verse. Jesus was tempted
in every way, and he can on a personal, visceral level feel and understand our struggle.

10. While grief is complex and confusing, one of the best resources to name our
whirlwinds and provide a helpful road map is David Kessler's work *Finding
Meaning: The Sixth Stage of Grief* (New York: Scribner, 2020).

11. Kenneth Savitski et al., "The Closeness-Communication Bias: Increased
Egocentrism Among Friends Versus Strangers," *Journal of Experimental Social
Psychology*, 47, no. 1 (January 2011): 269–73, https://www.sciencedirect.com
/science/article/abs/pii/S0022103110002118.

12. Dallas Willard, *The Spirit of the Disciples: Understanding How God Changes Lives*
(New York: HarperCollins, 1988), 210.

13. Zach Brittle, "Turn Towards Instead of Away," Gottman Institute, accessed August
1, 2022, https://www.gottman.com/blog/turn-toward-instead-of-away/.

14. I recommend reading Michael S. Sorensen, *I Hear You: The Surprisingly Simple
Skill Behind Extraordinary Relationships* (Lehi, UT: Autumn Creek Press, 2017).

Chapter 7: Practice #5: Accountability

1. Tim Keller (@timkellernyc), Twitter, April 30, 2014, 10:21 a.m., https://twitter
.com/timkellernyc/status/461525634758742016?lang=en.

2. Barna Research Release, "National Study Describes Christian Accountability
Provided by Churches," Barna Group, November 29, 2010, https://www
.barna.com/research/national-study-describes-christian-accountability
-provided-by-churches/.

3. Wherever you land on the textual criticism of John 7:51–8:11, as pastor and

theologian John Piper would say, the point of the story is still unshakably true. John Piper, "Neither Do I Condemn You," *Desiring God*, March 6, 2011, https://www.desiringgod.org/messages/neither-do-i-condemn-you--3.

4. Tim Keller (@timkellernyc), Twitter, May 28, 2019, 4:34 a.m., https://twitter.com/timkellernyc/status/1133305410855821312?lang=en.

5. Kevin DeYoung, "Full of Grace and Truth," Gospel Coalition, June 3, 2014, https://www.thegospelcoalition.org/blogs/kevin-deyoung/full-of-grace-and-truth/.

6. *Craig Ferguson: Does This Need to be Said?*, directed by Keith Truesdell (Los Angeles: Paramount Home Entertainment, DVD), 2011.

7. Ultimately, "each of us will give an account of himself to God" (Romans 14:12).

8. C. Stephen Evans, "Accountability Is Relational Responsibility," Templeton Religion Trust, last updated August 21, 2021, https://templetonreligiontrust.org/explore/accountability-is-relational-responsibility/.

9. "The Fear of the Lord and Virtue of Accountability," Regent College, streamed live on July 11, 2022, YouTube video, 1:54:32, https://www.youtube.com/watch?v=O5GKHGYLfyk.

Chapter 8: Being Fully Known and Truly Loved

1. Timothy Keller, *The Meaning of Marriage: Facing the Complexities of Commitment with the Wisdom of God* (New York: Penguin Books, 2011), 101.

2. Matthew McKay, Martha Davis, and Patrick Fanning, *Messages: The Communication Skills Book* (Oakland, CA: New Harbinger, 2009), 28.

3. M. Robert Mulholland Jr., "A Roadmap for Spiritual Formation," Transforming Center, 2016, https://transformingcenter.org/2016/05/nature-spiritual-formation/.

4. Dallas Willard, *Renovation of the Heart: Putting on the Character of Christ* (Colorado Springs: NavPress, 2002), 114.

Chapter 9: The Gift of Isolation

1. Allen Parr, "What to Do When You're Struggling with Loneliness," The Beat by Allen Parr, January 23, 2018, YouTube video, 7:19, https://www.youtube.com/watch?v=5eUElW81yDc.

2. Nouwen, *Bread for the Journey*, s.v. "August 14."

3. Jon Tyson, *Beautiful Resistance: The Joy of Conviction in a Culture of Compromise* (Colorado Springs: Multnomah, 2020).

Chapter 10: Cultivate Belonging in Christian Community

1. Daniel Grothe, *The Power of Place: Choosing Stability in a Rootless Age* (Nashville: Thomas Nelson, 2021).

2. Joseph Myers, *The Search to Belong: Rethinking Intimacy, Community, and Small Groups* (Grand Rapids: Zondervan, 2003), 36.

3. Brian Edgar, *God Is Friendship: A Theology of Spirituality, Community, and Society* (Franklin, TN: Seedbed, 2013).

4. Survey done on April 3, 2022: Out of 396 respondents, 157 chose "convenience," 145 "health-related concerns," 58 "personal/professional schedule conflict,"

21 "moved away but still would like to be connected," and 15 "not part of our community but still want to watch online."

5. Dietrich Bonhoeffer, *Life Together: The Classic Exploration of Faith in Community* (San Francisco: HarperOne, 1978), 27.

Conclusion

1. Joseph H. Hellerman, *When the Church Was a Family: Recapturing Jesus' Vision for Authentic Christian Community* (Nashville: B&H Academic, 2009), 1.

2. "The main thing that you bring the church is the person that you become." Dallas Willard, *Living in Christ's Presence: Final Words on Heaven and the Kingdom of God* (Downers Grove, IL: IVP, 2013), 106.

3. Andy Stanley, *Better Decisions, Fewer Regrets: 5 Questions to Help You Determine Your Next Move* (Grand Rapids: Zondervan, 2020), 145.

4. Flannery O'Connor, *The Habit of Being: Letters of Flannery O'Connor* (New York: Farrar, Straus & Giroux, 1988), 592.

About the Author

David Kim is the discipleship and formation pastor at WestGate Church in Silicon Valley, California. He is the author of a children's book about change, selected for Oprah's Favorite Things List in 2020. He completed his master of divinity and master of theology from Gordon-Conwell Theological Seminary and cares deeply about the intersection of spiritual formation, theology, and the cultivation of authentic Christian communities. He lives with his wife and two daughters in San Jose, California.